~ MYTHOLOGY ~

THE ILIAD AND THE ODYSSEY
IN
GREEK
MYTHOLOGY

Karen Bornemann Spies

Enslow Publishers, Inc.

40 Industrial Road	PO Box 38
Box 398	Aldershot
Berkeley Heights, NJ 07922	Hants GU12 6BP
USA	UK

http://www.enslow.com

*To Oz: for your advice, encouragement,
and friendship.*

Library of Congress Cataloging-in-Publication Data

Spies, Karen Bornemann.
    The Iliad and the Odyssey in Greek mythology / Karen Bornemann Spies.
       p. cm. — (Mythology)
    Summary: A retelling of the events of the Trojan War and the wanderings of
Odysseus based on Homer's Iliad and Odyssey. Includes explanatory notes
and review questions.
    Includes bibliographical references and index.
    ISBN 0-7660-1561-0 (hardcover)
    1. Trojan War—Juvenile literature. 2. Achilles (Greek mythology)—Juvenile
literature. 3. Odysseus (Greek mythology)—Juvenile literature. [1. Odysseus
(Greek mythology) 2. Achilles (Greek mythology) 3. Trojan War. 4. Mythology,
Greek.] I. Homer. Iliad. II. Homer. Odyssey. III. Title. IV. Mythology (Berkeley
Heights, N.J.)
    BL793.T7 S68 2002
    398.2'0938'02—dc21

                                          2001008261

Printed in the United States of America

10 9 8 7 6 5 4 3 2 1

To Our Readers: We have done our best to make sure all Internet addresses in
this book were active and appropriate when we went to press. However, the
author and the publisher have no control over and assume no liability for the
material available on those Internet sites or on other Web sites they may link to.
Any comments or suggestions can be sent by e-mail to comments@enslow.com
or to the address on the back cover.

Cover and illustrations by William Sauts Bock

⬚ CONTENTS ⬚

Map 4

Preface 5

1 The Judgment of Paris 16

2 Achilles Argues with Agamemnon 28

3 Achilles Versus Hector 44

4 The Trojan Horse 54

5 The Lotus-Eaters 66

6 The Cyclops 76

7 Circe, the Bewitching Queen 86

8 Deadly Dangers on the Sea 95

9 Home at Last 106

Glossary .118

Chapter Notes 120

Further Reading 124

Internet Addresses 125

Index 126

MAP of HOMER'S WORLD

MASK OF AGAMEMNON

PREFACE

People have told stories since the beginning of time. This book describes a certain type of story known as a myth. The word "myth" comes from the Greek word *mythos*, which means "word," "speech," or "story." Myths are traditional stories handed down by word of mouth. With each retelling, they may change slightly. Eventually, many myths are written down.

The myths in this book are a special type called epics. An epic is a long poem that narrates, or tells, the deeds of a hero or heroes. An epic uses elegant, formal language to tell of the bravery and mighty deeds of these heroes. However, an epic is more than just an entertaining tale of heroes and heroic deeds. An epic also describes the ideals of a culture at an important time in its history. Details of an epic may have a foundation in historical fact.

The epics in this book are based on the *Iliad* and the *Odyssey*. The poet Homer is commonly believed to have composed both poems in the late eighth or early seventh century B.C., even though no historical proof of his authorship exists. It is traditionally believed that Homer was born in the eighth century B.C. on Chios, an island in eastern Greece, or in Smyrna, a seaport in what is now western Turkey. The Greeks believed that he was a professional poet, and that he was blind. Both epic poems describe legendary events that the Greeks believed took place centuries before the poems were composed. This period was known as "the age of heroes." Homer wrote about the heroes and heroines of the *Iliad* and the *Odyssey* as a race of stronger and braver people than the Greeks of his day.

The *Iliad* recounts the story of the Trojan War, which may actually have taken place in about 1250 B.C. Supposedly, the

Greeks united under King Agamemnon of Mycenae in order to rescue Helen, the wife of his brother, King Menelaus of Sparta. The Trojan prince Paris had kidnapped Helen and taken her to Troy, a city in the western part of Asia Minor. The *Odyssey* describes the journey of the hero Odysseus after the end of the Trojan War. He encountered so many obstacles and adventures that it took him ten years to return to his home on the island of Ithaca, located off the western coast of mainland Greece. Many scholars thus consider the *Iliad* a poem about war and the *Odyssey* a postwar poem.[1]

These epics are important because they explore many universal concepts such as heroism. By reading these epics, we can learn how Greek ideals influenced other civilizations and their literature. Familiarity with these myths also helps us to understand many modern references described later in the book, such as Achilles' heel and the Trojan horse.

In this book, all references to the *Iliad* and the *Odyssey* are from the Robert Fagles translations listed in Further Reading. The first number refers to the book, or chapter, in the *Iliad* or *Odyssey* from which the quote is taken, followed by a period, and then the line number(s).

The World at the Time of the Iliad and the Odyssey

Ancient Greece was composed of the mainland and several surrounding islands, including Crete and Sicily. The mainland was located on the European continent east of Italy on the Mediterranean Sea. The Peloponnesus, a southern peninsula, was connected to the mainland by an isthmus near the ancient city of Corinth. Greek warriors in the *Iliad* came from cities in the Peloponnesus such as Mycenae, Sparta, Tiryns, Argos, and Pylos. Archaeologists have found evidence at these cities which supports Greek mythology about the kings who lived there, and have also found the remains of the magnificent palaces in which they dwelled.

Troy was situated in Asia Minor near the mouth of the

Hellespont, or Dardanelles, the waterway connecting Europe and Asia. This location allowed Troy to control much of the shipping in the ancient world. It is possible that the Greeks and Trojans fought the Trojan War over control of these shipping lanes. At the site of Troy, archaeologists have found evidence of several ruined cities, each one built atop the next. One was destroyed between 1250 and 1200 B.C., the period when the Trojan War supposedly took place. Unfortunately, it is not possible to determine if the city was destroyed by Greek invaders, an earthquake, or both. However, the presence of a number of cities at the same site is evidence that Troy commanded an important position.

In the *Odyssey*, Odysseus visits many mythical locations. However, his island home of Ithaca may have been the present-day island of the same name. Modern Ithaca is located in western Greece in the chain of Ionian Islands. It, like the Ithaca described in the *Odyssey*, is mountainous. It also has many archaeological relics of the time period of the Trojan War, so it may very well have been the site of the legendary kingdom of Odysseus.

Thousands of years ago, the Greeks had already gained fame as great seafarers who sailed throughout the Mediterranean. They carried on international trade in Asia Minor and Africa, Europe and the Middle East. Because of this, people from a variety of different backgrounds shared their myths with these Greek sailors. Many of the Greek myths we know today were adaptations of stories that the Greeks gleaned from these other cultures. The far-reaching voyages of the early Greeks help to explain the existence of different versions of each myth, and why the myths of many different cultures often resemble each other.

The Role of History

The history of ancient Greece influenced the development of the *Iliad* and the *Odyssey*, as well as Greek mythology as a whole. The earliest peoples migrated to the Greek mainland about 50,000 years ago from southwest Asia and from Africa. Little is known about the region until about 3000 B.C. The people, who lived in small villages, used bronze tools for farming and herding animals. They also used wheeled vehicles for transport.

In about 2000 B.C., tribes from the east came across Asia and built fortified towns on mainland Greece, where they subsisted by farming. At the same time, a powerful civilization developed on Crete. These people were known as the Minoans, after their king, Minos. The Minoans established a palatial civilization. Each palace was surrounded by homes for less wealthy people. The Minoans created a powerful seagoing empire and traded with cities on the other islands in the Aegean Sea, as well as with Sicily, Egypt, and cities on the eastern coast of the Mediterranean. The Minoan civilization was known for its international trade, sophisticated art, and fabulous wealth.

The Mycenaean Age (1600 B.C.–1200 B.C.)

By approximately 1600 B.C., civilization on mainland Greece became more powerful. The Greeks of this period, who are called the Mycenaeans, were named after the city of Mycenae. They are usually considered the "earliest Greeks," because they are the first residents known to have spoken Greek. The Mycenaeans developed a form of writing called Linear B, which they used for keeping accounts rather than for writing literature. Hence, myths from this period were still passed on orally.

A prosperous people, the Mycenaeans, like the Minoans, lived in independent communities built around palaces. The Mycenaeans, famed as fierce warriors, used bronze weapons and rode into battle in horse-drawn chariots. Because they frequently battled one another, the Mycenaeans protected their cities with strong walls. Although the *Iliad* and the *Odyssey* were written after this period, Homer set both epics during the Mycenaean Age. The bulk of the major Greek myths are connected with Mycenaean cities and heroes.[2]

In the 1870s, archaeologist Heinrich Schliemann excavated at Mycenae, where he discovered treasures such as masks of beaten gold, splendid jewelry, and weapons with intricate decorations. These discoveries provided evidence that there truly was a Mycenae "rich in gold," as Homer had described it in the *Iliad.* Schliemann also led the first excavations at Troy and continuing archaeological study has provided additional evidence of a powerful Mycenaean-age city there. Archaeologist Carl Blegen discovered a Mycenaean-age palace at Pylos. Many historians believe that this is the palace of Nestor, the wise warrior of the *Iliad.* Thus, archaeology has provided proof that cities and heroes described in the *Iliad* and the *Odyssey* actually existed. However, we must be careful to avoid assuming that every detail about the heroes and locations described in these myths is true.

At about the same time that Mycenaean civilization flourished, Minoan culture declined. Then, in about 1490 to 1470 B.C., the palaces on Crete were destroyed. Although historians remain uncertain as to what caused the ruins, archaeologists have located evidence of fire and massive destruction. The Mycenaeans may have invaded the island and destroyed its civilization or an earthquake may have caused the total destruction.

The Dark Age (1200 B.C.–800 B.C.)

The Mycenaean culture collapsed not long after the destruction of Troy at the end of the thirteenth century B.C. There are many possible causes of the demise of the Mycenaean civilization. These include earthquake; drought; social unrest within Mycenaean society; loss of trade contacts; and invasion of the Dorians, a group of Greek-speaking invaders from the north and east. In fact, the relatively sudden, extensive, and thorough eradication of Mycenaean palatial civilization is likely to have been caused by a combination of these factors. It was a gradual process spread over a full century to a century and a half following the destruction of the last palace.

The decline of Mycenaean culture ushered in a period in Greek history known as the "Dark Age." The elements that had made Greek civilization great, such as cities and palaces, art and the knowledge of writing, disappeared. Extensive migration occurred far beyond the boundaries of present-day Greece. Many historians believe that the epic stories of the return of the Greek heroes after the Trojan War, the *Nostoi*, portray these people movements. The strong rulers of the Mycenaean civilization had given way to a society organized around the family.

The Archaic Period (800 B.C.–475 B.C.)

The earliest examples of the Greek alphabet date from the last half of the eighth century B.C. The Greeks began to record poems, plays, and most of the stories that are now considered part of Greek mythology.

By about 750 B.C., the Greek city-state, or *polis*, came into existence. Each city-state was an independent, self-governing community which usually included the city and the surrounding rural area. Athens and Sparta were the most important city-states.

The city-states established colonies over a large area along the Mediterranean coasts and islands. Greek cities were established in Sicily and Italy, along the west coast of Asia Minor, and in the Black Sea region.

In 508 B.C., Athens became the first democracy in the world. The word "democracy" is based on the Greek words *demos*, "the people," and *kratein*, "to rule." Although Athens was a democracy, all of its people did not have the power to govern. Only citizens, defined as adult males who were born in Athens, were allowed to vote on issues related to governing the city-state. During this period, many Athenians owned slaves. Because women and slaves were not citizens, they were denied the right to vote.

The Classical Period (About 500 B.C.–338 B.C.)

This was the most famous period of ancient Greek civilization, a time when the Greeks reached their highest level of prosperity. Because of the leadership of the statesman Pericles, this period was termed "the Golden Age of Pericles." Greeks excelled in philosophy, art, literature, history, medicine, and government. Greek mythology flourished as poets recited myths at festivals and in the homes of the wealthy, and the works of Homer supplied the foundation of Greek education.

Athens was the center of most of these important developments. As a result, other city-states such as Sparta became jealous of Athens' power. In 431 B.C., the Peloponnesian War broke out between Sparta and Athens. After Athens ultimately lost the war in 404 B.C., the power of that city declined.

The Hellenistic Age (4th century B.C.–1st century B.C.)

Internal warfare continued among the Greeks until 338 B.C., when Philip of Macedon, a region in the northern part of Greece, conquered most of the Greek mainland. When Philip died, his son, Alexander, conquered additional territory. He provided a unified government for Asia Minor, Egypt, India, and Greece. However, after Alexander's sudden death at the age of thirty-three, his generals parceled out his empire among themselves. Still, even though Greece was politically divided, its cultural influence spread throughout all sections of society, especially since Greek was the language spoken at this time. What is known as Greek or Hellenistic influence continued for more than one thousand years.

Meanwhile, the power of Rome grew as the Romans conquered many tribes in Italy. By about 150 B.C., the Romans took control of Greece. They showed their respect for Greek culture by adopting many of its aspects, such as Greek art and literature. Although the Romans changed the names of many of the Greek gods, they adopted most of the Greek myths.

Religion and Culture

The Greeks believed in many gods and goddesses, which made them what is known as a polytheistic culture. They thought that the gods lived on Mount Olympus, an actual mountain in Thessaly, a region in north central Greece. According to legend, the gods could take on human form, leave their mountain home, and travel anywhere. The Greek gods felt human emotions such as anger, joy, and jealousy. Each god controlled at least one part of human life. For example, Zeus, king of the gods, was the god of thunder and ruled the sky.

The personalities and characteristics of the gods were not clearly defined until Homer wrote the *Iliad* and the *Odyssey*.[3] He portrayed the gods with vivid language. In the Homeric epics, the Olympian gods take sides in the war and even fight in some of the battles.

In particular, the gods react when the Homeric heroes show too much pride, or *hubris*. In the *Iliad*, both Achilles and Agamemnon refuse to give in to each other during their argument. This excessive pride directly influences the course of the Trojan War.

The role of the gods in the fate of mankind is another important part of the epics. Fate is the concept that life's outcomes are predetermined. Usually Zeus controlled human destiny. He handed out his decisions through the Fates, three of his daughters. The fate of the heroes Achilles and Hector is already set at the beginning of the epics. However, even though the gods were so powerful, they, too, were subject to fate. For example, in the *Iliad*, Zeus could not prevent the death of his own son, Sarpedon.

The "Homeric Question"

These epics are now nearly 3,000 years old. Yet, they are still the subjects of scholarly debate over the "Homeric question," which is actually a series of questions. Was Homer the author of the *Iliad* and the *Odyssey*? When were these epics written down? How were they composed? No archeological evidence exists to definitely answer these questions. However, the ancient Greeks believed that Homer was the author of the poems.[4] Many modern scholars note that both the *Iliad* and the *Odyssey* have a total overall unity. These scholars believe that this unity proves that both poems had to be written by the same person.

However, other historians believe that the epics could not have been composed at one time by the same individual. Rather, they are collections of shorter *lays*, or simple narrative poems. These lays were combined to form the longer epic poem.

Modern scholars believe that the *Iliad* and the *Odyssey* are based on a long tradition of oral poetry.[5] Both epics use repetition in phrases, word groups, and scenes. For example, the hero Achilles is repeatedly referred to as "godlike" and "swift-footed." The god Apollo is "one who shoots from afar." Common actions such as eating a meal or fighting a duel are described in a similar fashion. These repetitious phrases and scenes, or verbal formulas, were developed over the years by many ancient Greek poets. Since writing was not yet in use, the poets had to perform without using a written poem. Instead of memorizing many poems, they gradually learned these verbal formulas. With practice, the poets added more formulas to the collection they had memorized. They could then combine various scenes and phrases to improvise, thus creating long epic poems with little preparation.

But other historians point out that such a view ignores the magnificent scope and beautiful language of Homer's work. Also, certain repeated phrases flow so poetically that they must have been intentionally created this way, not developed by a verbal formula.[6] An in-depth examination of certain types of scenes, such as a warrior arming for battle, has shown that none of the scenes are exactly alike. Even though some of the phrases within them are repeated, the scenes differ.[7] All these points make it difficult to believe that Homer depended on oral formulas and did not know how to write. However, there is enough repetition in his work that scholars agree that Homer's work was based on a long tradition of oral poetry.[8] He then used the new technique of writing to refine and lengthen the poem. Most likely, such an effort took his entire lifetime.[9]

The epics were preserved in writing at the beginning of the ninth century B.C. after the development of the Greek alphabet. Painstakingly, they were hand-copied onto rolls of papyrus, an Egyptian plant cut into strips and pressed to make a paper-type material.[10] Each book, or chapter, into which the *Iliad* and the *Odyssey* is divided may have originally been transcribed onto a single roll. From the second to fifth centuries A.D., the materials used to copy the books changed dramatically. Parchment pages bound into books replaced papyrus rolls. For 1,000 years after that, Homer's works were scribed by hand onto paper or vellum, a fine-grained animal skin. The first machine-printed edition of the epics appeared in Florence, Italy, in 1488, and used a form of type that imitated Greek handwriting. Countless translations of Homer have been printed since then.

The *Iliad* and the *Odyssey* are the first poems written in Greek literature. As such, they are usually considered the oldest complete books of western civilization.[11] Their rich, flowing poetry and colorful, heroic stories are a legacy worthy of continued reading and study.

1

THE JUDGMENT OF PARIS

INTRODUCTION

The story of the Trojan War has attracted generations of scholars, archaeologists, and the general public, all of whom would like to prove that the war actually took place. We may never know for sure the relationship between the myths told of Troy and its actual existence. Still, whatever its foundation in historical fact, the Trojan War is considered by many historians and mythologists to be the most important story to have survived in Greek mythology.[1]

We do know, however, that the poems of Homer and the other bards, or composers of epics, are not history. Rather, they are stories in a historical setting, developed about the emotions of human beings and the choices they face in life. The sometimes tragic results of human choices make for fascinating reading.

The events leading up to the war and those which follow it are known as the Trojan Cycle. The *Iliad* and the *Odyssey* make up an important part of the cycle of stories. Other parts of it must be constructed from many later stories, including those of Greek playwrights of the fifth century B.C. and Roman writers who followed them.

According to legend, the mighty city of Troy flourished more than three thousand years ago. The Greeks and Trojans went to war over the city. The war started because Paris, a prince of Troy, kidnapped Helen, the wife of King Menelaus of Sparta, and took her to Troy. Menelaus then called upon all the kings and princes of the Greek world to join him in capturing Helen and bringing her back to Troy. The seeds of the war grew from a dispute between three jealous goddesses, Athena, Hera, and Aphrodite. Their story is told in the myth, "The Judgment of Paris."

Homer refers to the myth about the judgment of Paris and its influence on the beginning of the war in Book 24 of the *Iliad*. His reference makes it clear that the myth was well known to Homer's audience.[2] The following retelling of "The

Judgment of Paris" is taken from two other sources. One is the *Trojan Women*, a play by Euripides, a playwright who wrote at the same time as Homer. The other source is Lucian's *Dialogues*. Lucian was a Syrian author who was born in about A.D. 120. "The Judgment of Paris" makes clear how the Trojan War started.

An important part of this myth is the tradition of *xenia*, or guest-friendship, which the Greeks valued. Hospitality was always offered to a guest. Both guest and host were bound to help each other. Menelaus trusted Paris completely. However, Paris broke this sacred bond when he kidnapped Helen.

Helen plays an important part in the "The Judgment of Paris." Because of her, the war was fought. She ran off with Paris, leaving behind her husband and nine-year-old daughter. She did this without considering the consequences of her actions on others. Although Helen was considered the most beautiful woman in the world, she was not happy. She became bored with the vanity of Paris and his lack of bravery compared to Hector, his brother. The Trojans, except for Priam, Paris, and Hector, grew to hate Helen because of her role in the cause of the Trojan War.

THE JUDGMENT OF PARIS

Peleus, king of the Phthia, and Thetis, a sea nymph, were deeply in love. When they planned their wedding feast, they decided not to invite Eris, the goddess of Discord, who always caused problems. On the day of the wedding, all the other Olympian gods gathered in happiness to celebrate the marriage. Eris, furious that she was the only Olympian who had been left out, decided to live up to her name and cause trouble. Into the midst of the wedding banquet hall, she tossed an apple with the words *May the Most Beautiful Goddess Take It* inscribed on it.

Hera, Aphrodite, and Athena each claimed the apple for herself.

"Surely as the queen of the gods, I deserve this wonderful fruit," said Hera, as she snatched the apple off the floor.

Aphrodite tried to grab the apple from Hera. "No, as the goddess of beauty, I must claim the prize."

Powerful Athena wrestled them for the apple as well. "I am both regal and powerful. The apple must be mine!"

"Zeus, my husband, you must choose," said Hera, confident that he would select her.

Aphrodite nodded. "Yes, in your wisdom, you are the only one who can make the correct decision."

"Mighty Zeus, since you are king of the gods, we must abide by your choice," added Athena. Because Zeus was her father, Athena was certain he would rule in her favor, especially if she honored him with her comments.

Zeus, however, decided not to settle the dispute himself. "I love all three of you equally. It is impossible that I could choose among you." Zeus knew that these three goddesses had strong tempers. Whoever did not receive the apple would be angry with him, and he did not want to feel the wrath of the other two strong-willed goddesses.

"Go ask Paris, the Trojan prince. He is known as an excellent judge of beauty," said Zeus. "He lives on Mount Ida, where he keeps his father's sheep."

Hera frowned. "You wish for a lowly shepherd to decide among three goddesses?"

"Paris is the son of Priam, king of Troy," Zeus said. "He must live on the mountain for a seer prophesied that he would cause the destruction of the city." Zeus handed the apple to Hermes, his winged messenger. Zeus instructed Hermes to tell Paris that he had been chosen to make this important decision because he was so handsome himself and known far and wide as a wise judge in matters of beauty and love.

Hermes flew off with the three goddesses toward Mount Ida, telling them about the young man as they traveled. "Paris is sometimes called Alexander, which means 'warder-off-of-men,'" said Hermes. "He is so strong that he once single-handedly drove off a band of robbers. He is so strong that we

do not want to sneak up on him and risk attack." Hermes swept down from the sky with the goddesses and landed on the mountain some distance away from Paris. As they approached him, they awoke the young hero from a nap.

"Who are these marvelous beauties who stand before me, Hermes?" asked Paris, who himself was stunningly handsome.

Hermes whispered to Paris the names of the goddesses. As he described the awesome task facing the young prince, the messenger god handed the apple to Paris.

"May the Most Beautiful Goddess Take It," read Paris. "Hermes, how am I, a mere mortal and a man who lives in the fields, to choose among these three visions of loveliness? Their beauty surrounds me totally."

"I am not sure how to choose, yet you must obey an order from Zeus," answered the messenger god.

Paris asked one thing of Hermes: to convince the two goddesses who did not receive the apple to look upon him kindly. "Ask them not to hold their defeat against me. Let them realize that their defeat was in my eyes, not in their wondrous beauty."

The goddesses agreed not to blame Paris. But one by one, they each offered him a bribe to be chosen as the most beautiful. Hera promised to give Paris control over all of the world. Athena, goddess of war and wisdom, would grant Paris victory in all his battles. 2Aphrodite, goddess of beauty, promised to give Paris the most beautiful woman in the world.

Paris could not resist Aphrodite's promise, so he chose her as the fairest goddess. Aphrodite then told Paris that he could have the world's loveliest woman: Helen. Unfortunately, Aphrodite did not tell Paris that Helen was already married.

Helen was so beautiful that every prince and hero of Greece had wanted to marry her. Rich and powerful suitors had come from every corner of Greece to bid for Helen's hand in marriage. Her father, King Tyndareus, feared that the suitors he did not choose would unite against him. He made them all promise to agree to his decision as to who would be Helen's husband. Furthermore, all the suitors had to promise to come to the aid of Helen's husband if any wrong was ever done to him because of his marriage to Helen. After the suitors swore to abide by King Tyndareus' choice, he selected Menelaus, king of Sparta, to marry Helen.

Because Helen was already married to Menelaus, the only way Paris could win her was by stealing her away from her husband. Paris went to Sparta, where Menelaus welcomed him, as was the custom of the ancient Greeks. Menelaus had no suspicion of Paris' plan to kidnap his wife.

One day, Menelaus had to leave Sparta to go to a funeral on the island of Crete. As soon as Menelaus left, Paris spirited

Helen away to Troy. As soon as Helen had cast her eyes upon the handsome young prince, she was attracted to him. She forgot about her marriage vows to Menelaus and went willingly with Paris to his home across the sea.

When Menelaus returned, he learned immediately that Helen was gone. The mighty king was so furious that he called upon all of her former suitors to help him, as they had promised to do. Kings, princes, and great heroes came from all over Greece to go with Menelaus to Troy to get back his wife. Menelaus would make Paris and Troy pay for the loss of Helen. The Trojan War was about to begin.

QUESTIONS AND ANSWERS

Q: What was the main cause of the Trojan War?

A: Three jealous goddesses (Hera, Athena, and Aphrodite) argued over which of them was the fairest.

Q: Who did Zeus ask to settle this dispute and why?

A: He asked Paris, prince of Troy, who was considered a great judge of beauty. Zeus did not want to become involved because such action would make the goddesses angry with him.

Q: Which goddess did Paris choose as the fairest and what did she promise him?

A: He selected Aphrodite, who promised Paris the most beautiful woman in the world.

Q: Who was the most beautiful woman? What was the problem with Paris marrying her?

A: Helen, the most lovely woman, was already the wife of King Menelaus of Sparta.

Q: How did Paris win Helen? What tradition did his action violate?

A: He visited Sparta and stole her away when Menelaus was not there. This action violated the custom of xenia, or guest-friendship. Hospitality was always offered to a guest. Both guest and host were bound to help each other.

Q: What did Menelaus do when he returned to find that Helen was gone?

A: He called upon all of her former suitors to hold to their promise to help him.

EXPERT COMMENTARY

The first city described in Greek literature is Troy. According to Bernard Knox, a scholar of Greek history:

> The Greek *polis*, the city-state, was a community surrounded by potential enemies, who could turn into actual belligerents at the first sign of aggression or weakness. The permanence of war is a theme echoed in Greek literature from Homer to Plato.[3]

Knox further noted the importance of the city-state:

> The city, the *polis*, as the Greeks called it, was for them the matrix of civilization, the only form of ordered social life they could understand; it is the exclusive form assumed by ancient Greek culture from its beginning to its end. The city was small enough so that the citizens knew one another, participated in a communal life, shared the common joy of festivals, the sorrow of public bereavement, and keen excitement of competition, the common heritage of ancestral tombs and age-old sanctified places. The destruction of a city is a calamity all the more deeply felt because of the close cohesion of its inhabitants and their attachment, reinforced over generations from a mythical past, to its landmarks and buildings.[4]

Knox pointed out that Troy was a particularly fine example of the polis because:

> It is a site chosen with an eye to defensive capabilities, with a high eminence that serves as a citadel, a sacred area for the temples and palaces. It is near the junction of two rivers, and it depends on the produce of the surrounding plain, which is rich plowland and grows wheat. It is fortified against attackers: it is well-walled and well-built, it has steep ramparts and gates. These fortifications enclose a vision of civilized life, the splendors of wealth and peace.[5]

It was no wonder that the Greeks hoped to win not only Helen, but a share of these riches.

According to myth, Helen and Menelaus had a daughter,

Hermione. By abusing the hospitality of Menelaus, Paris caused Helen to make a crucial choice:

> Menelaus received Paris warmly, according to the conventions of *xenia*, "guest friendship." When Menelaus was called to Crete to attend a funeral, Paris and Helen, irresistibly attracted to one another, gathered up the treasure in the palace and eloped. Thus Helen left behind her lawful husband, her nine-year-old daughter, Hermione, and her good name—such is the power of Aphrodite.[6]

As the *Iliad* develops, Hera, the wife of Zeus, and Athena, his daughter, demonstrate a powerful hatred toward Troy. The reason for the hatred is not explained until Book 24, when Homer refers to the Judgment of Paris. According to Bernard Knox:

> It seems clear from the casual, almost cryptic, way Homer refers to the story that it was perfectly familiar to his audience, and Hera's motive for hating Troy, the insult to her beauty, is perfectly consonant with the picture of Hera as the jealous divine wife Homer presents elsewhere in the *Iliad*—in her plot against Heracles, Zeus's child by a mortal woman (14.300-8), and her brutal assault on Artemis, Zeus's child by another goddess (21.557-66). . . . And this personal motive has its opposite side: the unfailing support given to the Trojans by the winner of the beauty contest, Aphrodite, and her intervention to save Paris from his fate at the hands of Menelaus (3.439-41).[7]

2

ACHILLES ARGUES WITH AGAMEMNON

INTRODUCTION

Agamemnon, the commander of the Greek forces during the Trojan War, quarrelled with Achilles, his greatest warrior. They argued violently over the spoils, or prizes, of war. Agamemnon had taken away Briseïs, a slave girl whom Achilles had won. The Greeks considered war prizes to be evidence of a hero's honor. Thus, Agamemnon's action slighted Achilles' honor.

The story of Achilles and Agamemnon is told in the *Iliad*, which is divided into twenty-four parts called books. In Homer's day, the *Iliad* was recited at festivals, where it took two or three days to perform, because it required fifteen sessions of two hours each.[1] Most likely, poets took turns reciting it.

Iliad is a word which means "a poem about Ilium." *Ilium* was another name for the city of Troy. However, the *Iliad* is not just about the city of Troy and the Trojan War. The first line of Homer's epic notes that the poem's subject is:

> *"Rage—Goddess, sing the rage of Peleus' son*
> *Achilles..."*(1.1)[2]

The rage, or fierce anger, of Achilles occurred after the quarrel he had with Agamemnon. Their quarrel took place in the tenth and last year of the Trojan War. As a result of his rage, Achilles acted unheroically by withdrawing from the battle. His pride, or *hubris*, got in the way of his duty as a warrior. His actions caused the deaths of many warriors, both Trojan and Greek. However, Achilles finally became aware of how his pride had caused his inappropriate actions. This awareness—and his fated death—make him a tragic hero.

At that time, there was no unified Greek nation. Rather, there were many cities, each with its own king and ruling family. Homer referred to the Greek fighting forces as "the Achaeans." Achaea was a region in the northern

Peloponnesus. According to Greek mythology, the Achaeans were descended from Achaeus, the grandson of Hellen. Hellen was the ancestor of the Hellenes, another name for the Greeks. Ancient Greece was known as Hellas.

The Greek and Trojan armies were organized differently. The Greeks were led by King Agamemnon of Mycenae, the brother of Menelaus. However, the army he commanded was made up of smaller independent groups, or contingents. Each contingent had its own commander. Achilles, for example, commanded the Myrmidons. At any time, a commander could withdraw his independent army from the fighting, which Achilles did for a time.

Troy was a powerful city led by a mighty king, Priam. His fifty sons, including Paris and Hector, were part of that army. Troy also received help from independent allies from different nations. These allies included the Amazons, a mighty race of warrior women; the Ethiopians, from the south; and the Lycians, from southern Asia Minor. When Homer compared the Trojans and Greeks, he considered the Trojans more cosmopolitan, or having a world-wide mixture.[3]

The war took place in Troy and the area surrounding it. In the 1870s, archaeologist Heinrich Schliemann went in search of the site of the ancient city. He excavated what is known as the mound of Hissarlik. This mound is located on the plain by the Hellespont (Dardanelles) in the northwest corner of present-day Turkey. There, Schliemann found evidence of at least nine cities, layered one atop the other. These cities are referred to as Troy 1, Troy 2, and so on. Schliemann believed that Troy 2 was the location of the city where the Trojan War took place. He based his claims on the jewelry and golden treasure that he found there. However, modern archaeologists believe that the mythical city was either Troy 6 or Troy 7, because these ruins are dated closer to the time the war is believed to have occurred.

The power and tragedy of war are a key theme of Homer's *Iliad*. Ever since Homer wrote his epic, war has been one of the most powerful themes in literature. Homer does not show war as glorious, although he does describe how it can bring out in warriors their greatest efforts.

Achilles represents an important concept in the *Iliad*, that of *arete*, or excellence. To Homer, a warrior's arete was linked to his skill in battle and to the amount of war prizes he won. War supplied the perfect opportunity to display arete and earn glory, or *kleos*. Many Greeks, including Achilles, went to Troy because they knew they would win glory there. A warrior was filled with a sense of duty to always try to do his best. When Agamemnon took away part of Achilles' spoils of war, he diminished Achilles' arete.

Stories that do not appear in the *Iliad* provide important background for events that take place in the epic. Achilles' mother, the sea nymph Thetis, did not want her son to fight in the war. A prophecy foretold that Achilles would die if he went to Troy. If he did not, Achilles would live a long, full life. When Achilles was born, legend told that Thetis tried to make him immortal. She held him by the heel and dipped him in the river Styx, which flowed through the Underworld, the place the Greeks believed people went when they died. Everywhere the water touched Achilles became invulnerable. However, the water never touched the spot on Achilles' heel where his mother had held him. Thus, Achilles' heel was left vulnerable, and he would eventually die of a wound to this heel. His death is foretold in the *Iliad* in Book 19 and the ghost of Achilles appears to Odysseus in Book 15 of the *Odyssey*. The term *Achilles' heel* now refers to any weak or vulnerable spot.

Another story provides valuable information about events occurring in the *Iliad*. The mighty Greek fleet gathered at Aulis, preparing to sail to Troy, but the ships could not leave while the north winds blew. Day after day, the north winds raged with no end in sight.

Agamemnon consulted Calchas, the prophet, who revealed that Agamemnon had angered Artemis, the goddess of the hunt, by boasting that he was a better hunter than she. To save the expedition, Agamemnon would have to sacrifice his daughter, Iphigenia. Agamemnon tricked Iphigenia into coming to Aulis. He wrote home to his wife that he had arranged for Iphigenia to marry Achilles. When Iphigenia arrived, expecting to be a bride, she was put to death instead. The north winds stopped immediately, and the ships set sail, ready to wage war.

ACHILLES ARGUES WITH AGAMEMNON

The Greeks had spent nine years warring with the people of Troy. They had also attacked cities in the surrounding countryside. Whenever they won such battles, they collected booty, or treasure, from the people they defeated and made slaves of women they had captured. After one battle, Agamemnon received as a prize of war a young woman named Chryseïs. Her father, Chryses, was a priest of Apollo. Chryses approached the Greek camp, bearing priceless gifts that he hoped Agamemnon would accept in exchange for releasing his daughter.

"Agamemnon, may the gods of Olympus give you Priam's city of Troy to plunder," the old priest begged. "Please, accept these gifts as ransom for my daughter, and honor the god I serve, mighty Apollo."

Agamemnon, who had no intention of giving up Chryseïs, dismissed the priest with an angry order. "Never again, old man, let me catch sight of you by our ships or our camp!"

Chryses fled to a safe place by the seashore. He prayed, "Hear me, Apollo! If ever I served you well, repay me by punishing Agamemnon and his troops."

His prayer went up to Olympus, where Apollo heard him. Down from the mighty mountain came the god of war with his bow and quiver of arrows. He knelt down on one knee and shot one arrow after another at the Greeks from his silver bow, for nine days in a row. Every time an arrow hit, it spread pestilence throughout the army, killing many warriors.

Achilles called together the leaders of the Greek expedition. "We cannot fight against both disease and the Trojans. Perhaps we are beaten and the campaign lost. But let us first consult with the prophet Calchas. This holy man may reveal why Apollo rages so against us."

Calchas knew that Agamemnon would dislike his prophecy, so he asked Achilles to save him from Agamemnon's anger. "Apollo sends down his deadly arrows because Agamemnon has angered him by sending away his priest. The king ignored Chryses' ransom and refused to return his daughter."

Agamemnon stood, his eyes blazing with fury, and turned upon the prophet. "Never do your prophecies favor me! Now you say I must give up Chryseïs! I am willing to give her back if that will be best for my troops. Just bring me another prize in her place." Agamemnon felt that he would be disgraced if he did not have a war prize as wonderful as Chryseïs.

Achilles quickly answered. "Just how, Agamemnon, can you receive another prize now? All our treasures captured in war have been given out to the rank and file of our troops. Should we force one of them to give up his prize? That would be truly disgraceful."

Agamemnon accused Achilles of selfishness. "Would you keep your own prize while I sit here empty-handed? No, if I have to give up Chryseïs, I will take your prize of war, the young woman Briseïs, as my own, just to show you how much greater I am than you!"

Achilles fell into a rage, determined to draw his sword and slay Agamemnon for this slight to his honor. "See here, you scoundrel," he raged at Agamemnon. "Even though you command our forces, you have no right to take my war prize. Whenever we battle our foe, you already take more booty for yourself. Yet I have always done more of the actual fighting. By rights, I deserve all of the booty I have received and more."

Agamemnon replied, "I am the commander of these

forces. I care not what you do, nor do I fear your rage. I shall keep Briseïs."

A furious Achilles stormed off to his tents where his friend, Patroclus, waited along with the rest of Achilles' troops, who were known as the Myrmidons. Achilles commanded Patroclus to surrender Briseïs to Agamemnon's men. But because his anger against the king had not lessened, Achilles withdrew from all the fighting and stayed in his tent. He forbid the Myrmidons to fight under any other commander.

Thetis, Achilles' mother, was as furious with Agamemnon as was her son. "Have nothing more to do with the Greeks, my son," said Thetis. "I shall go up to Mount Olympus where the gods reside and speak on your behalf to Zeus, the king of all the gods." Thetis asked Zeus to give success not to the Greeks, but to the Trojans. In this way, she hoped that Agamemnon would suffer for the dishonor and anger he had caused her son.

Zeus decided to favor Thetis' plea. He knew that without Achilles, the Greeks had no chance of defeating the Trojans. That night, Zeus sent to Agamemnon a dream that was untrue. The dream foretold that the Greeks would win if he attacked.

The next day, Achilles remained in his tent while the Greeks fought fiercely, with neither side winning. Suddenly the fighting stopped, and the armies drew apart. Two warriors—the Trojan, Paris, and the Greek, Menelaus—faced each other. The two would fight each other to the death to determine the outcome of the battle.

Paris struck at Menelaus with his spear, but Menelaus pushed the spear back with his shield. Menelaus then hurled his own spear. It tore Paris' tunic, but did not wound him. Menelaus quickly drew his sword, but it mysteriously fell from his hand, broken in pieces. Quickly, Menelaus jumped on top of Paris and grabbed the strap of his helmet. He began to drag Paris back to the Greek camp. However, Aphrodite helped

Paris. She tore away the strap of the helmet, so that Menelaus lost hold of Paris.

Then, Aphrodite caught Paris up in a cloud and took him back to Troy. He remained safely behind the walls of Troy, relaxing with Helen, while Hector and the rest of the Trojans prepared to fight on.

Agamemnon announced to both the Greeks and the Trojans that Menelaus had won the fight between Menelaus and Paris. He insisted that the Trojans give Helen back to Menelaus. The Trojans were about to agree, for they did not respect Paris. A true warrior would not hide behind the city walls with a woman while his comrades went into battle. Then, Hera and Athena tricked a Trojan warrior into shooting an arrow at Menelaus, and the Greeks fought back in a heightened rage.

At the same time, Zeus recalled his promise to Thetis to avenge the wrongs done to Achilles. Zeus ordered the rest of the gods to stay in Olympus. He went down to the battlefield and helped Hector fight with brilliance. One Greek warrior after another fell beneath his mighty spear. By nightfall, the Trojans had driven the Greeks back to their ships.

That night, the Trojans celebrated, while the Greeks pondered their fate. Agamemnon was all for sailing back to Greece. Nestor, the oldest and wisest of the commanders, spoke out against Agamemnon. He criticized him for his treatment of Achilles. "If you, my great Agamemnon, had not angered Achilles, we would not now have suffered such defeats," Nestor said. "How can you tame his anger and convince him to rejoin us once again?"

The Greeks cheered at Nestor's advice. Agamemnon admitted that he had acted in a selfish manner. "I will send Briseïs back to Achilles with my best messengers," Agamemnon said. "And with her, I will send many gifts of great splendor, treasures certain to convince Achilles to join us again." Agamemnon carefully chose his messengers: Odysseus, who was glib of tongue; Nestor, the wisest and most experienced of the Greek warriors; Ajax, the brave fighter; and Phoenix, a priest of Zeus who was almost like a father to Achilles.

Achilles, along with his closest friend, Patroclus, welcomed the messengers into his tent. "Make yourselves comfortable," Achilles said. "Patroclus, bring a bigger wine bowl and mix a stronger wine." Achilles carved up and served juicy meats, while Patroclus also brought bread.

Then, Odysseus addressed Achilles. "Mighty Achilles, Agamemnon will fill your ship with gold and bronze from the spoils of Troy, if only you will rejoin us in battle. He offers you the hand of any of his daughters in marriage and seven cities as marriage gifts. And of course, Briseïs will be yours. I ask you to consider the fate of your fellow Greeks, who are weary from fighting. Even if you cannot find it in your heart to forgive Agamemnon, will you not consider helping your comrades in arms?"

"I have no need of the treasures Agamemnon offers, for indeed, they are like bribery," Achilles said. "I will marry no daughter of Agamemnon. And though he claims to be a mighty warrior, Agamemnon is shameless in that he will not even make his request to me face-to-face. All the treasures of Egypt would not convince me to rejoin him. In fact, tomorrow at dawn, I shall sail home."

Achilles' response astounded Odysseus and the other messengers. Phoenix spoke out. "Sail home? Is this the plan you have been hatching, Achilles? Have you no courage left? I, who have treated you like a son, have never given you the advice to run from danger."

And so, Agamemnon's messengers brought him word that Achilles' proud spirit had overruled his love for his fellow warriors and that he refused to join the Greeks in battle. All during the night, Agamemnon struggled over what to do. Should the Greeks fight on or should they leave Troy in disgrace? Agamemnon tore at his hair, unable to sleep. Finally, he sought the counsel of Nestor. Together, they roused all the warriors. With Nestor's advice adding weight to

Agamemnon's words, the Greeks decided to go into battle against the Trojans the next day.

Clad in armor of gleaming bronze, Agamemnon led his troops. Although they fought with great courage, the Greeks lost many warriors. Slashed by a sharp spear, Agamemnon returned to his ship to tend his wounds. When Hector saw that Agamemnon was no longer fighting, he rallied his men and drove the Greeks back to the very beaches where their ships were moored.

From his camp, Achilles watched the fighting, certain that the Achaeans would again beg him to rejoin the battle. He sent Patroclus to ask Nestor which Greeks had suffered wounds.

"Why does Achilles seek word of his comrades when he will not even help them in battle?" Nestor asked Patroclus. The wise old warrior knew that Achilles was only searching for bad news about the Greeks.

Patroclus, though he remained friendly to Achilles, could no longer bear to watch the Greeks suffer such huge losses. He begged Achilles to lend him his armor. "If the Trojans see your armor," Patroclus said, "they may confuse me for you. They may let up in their fierce fighting."

Achilles agreed to his friend's request. "As a man dishonored, I will not fight unless the battle comes near my own ships. But you may take my armor. And I will order my troops to follow you into battle. Just do not go near the walls of Troy, where Hector is strongest. I wish you well, my friend."

Patroclus donned the gleaming armor of the mighty Achilles. The Trojans recognized it right away and fled in fear, because they thought that Achilles had rejoined the Greeks. At first, Patroclus fought with all the valor of his friend. He led the Myrmidons bravely, even killing Sarpedon, son of Zeus.

But Patroclus forgot the warning of Achilles and came near the slope leading to the walls of Troy, where Apollo stood. Three times Patroclus charged the high wall and three times Apollo hurled him back. The fourth time, Apollo cried out with words of terror, "Go back, Patroclus. Fate has not willed that the walls of Troy fall before your spear."

As Patroclus backed away, Apollo whispered to Hector. "Why stop your fighting now? This is your chance to drive the Greeks into the sea. Drive your chariot straight at Patroclus. I, Apollo, shall give you glory!"

Hector whipped his stallions into a fury, and they charged at Patroclus. Apollo knocked Patroclus' helmet off his head. As Patroclus, dazed, fell toward the ground, Hector rammed him with his spear. Horror filled the Achaeans as they realized that the armor of Achilles had not been enough to protect Patroclus.

As Patroclus struggled to breathe, he warned Hector, "Even now as I lay dying, know that you, too, shall soon follow me in death. Already I see the strong force of fate rising up to bring you down at the hands of Achilles!" Then Patroclus breathed his last, and his soul flew down to Hades, the land of the dead.

Hector stood over the body of Patroclus, planted his heel on Patroclus' chest, and pulled out his spear. He stripped Achilles' armor from Patroclus' body and put it on himself. As Hector put on the armor, Zeus watched and foretold his doom:

> *Poor soldier. Never a thought of death weighs down*
> *your spirit now, yet death is right beside you. . .*
> *You don the deathless arms of a great fighter—*
> *and all other fighters tremble before him, true,*
> *but you, you killed his comrade, gentle, strong. . .*
> *never again will you return from battle,*
> *Hector. . . .*(17.230-238) [4]

QUESTIONS AND ANSWERS

Q: *What caused the quarrel between Agamemnon and Achilles?*

A: Achilles called for the Greek army leaders to meet to convince Agamemnon to let Chryseïs go. Agamemnon was furious that he had to give up the girl, so he took for himself Achilles' slave girl, Briseïs.

Q: *How did Achilles react to Agamemnon's action?*

A: Achilles was so angry with Agamemnon that he withdrew from the fighting and refused to let his troops fight with the Greeks.

Q: *After Achilles withdrew from the fighting, which two warriors faced each other in one-on-one combat? What happened?*

A: Menelaus and Paris fought as their armies watched. Just as Menelaus was about to drag Paris back to the Greek camp, Aphrodite rescued Paris.

Q: *What did Agamemnon offer Achilles in return for coming back? How did Achilles answer?*

A: Agamemnon offered rich treasure and the return of Briseïs. Achilles was insulted, because he considered Agamemnon's offer to be bribery. He refused to rejoin the Greeks.

Q: *Which warrior then wore Achilles' armor and what happened to him?*

A: Patroclus borrowed the armor of Achilles and led the Myrmidons into battle. At first, the Greeks were winning. Then, Hector killed Patroclus and put on Achilles' armor.

EXPERT COMMENTARY

Although some historians may have expressed doubts about the actual existence of Troy and the Trojan War, according to translator Robert Fagles:

> . . . the Greeks of historic times who knew and loved Homer's poem had none. For them history began with a splendid Panhellenic expedition against an Eastern foe, led by kings and including contingents from all the more than one hundred and fifty places listed in the catalogue in Book 2. History began with a war. That was an appropriate beginning, for the Greek city-states, from their first appearance as organized communities until the loss of their political independence, were almost uninterruptedly at war with one another.[5]

Fagles also noted that Homer's epic examined the effects of war on the individual:

> The *Iliad* accepts violence as a permanent factor in human life and accepts it without sentimentality, for it is just as sentimental to pretend that war does not have its monstrous ugliness as it is to deny that it has its own strange and fatal beauty, a power, which can call out in men resources of endurance, courage and self-sacrifice that peacetime, to our sorrow and loss, can rarely command. Three thousand years have not changed the human condition in this respect; we are still lovers and victims of the will to violence, and so long as we are, Homer will still be read as its truest interpreter.[6]

Achilles is the main character in Homer's *Iliad* and his temper is evident at the beginning. His life was destined to end prematurely, according to writer and publisher Roberto Calasso:

> Instead of a god who would live longer than other gods, he became a man who would have a shorter life than other men. And yet, of all men, he was the closest to being a god. . . . Achilles is time in its purest state, drumming hooves galloping away. Compressed into the piercing fraction of a mortal life span, he came closest to having the qualities the Olympians

lived and breathed: intensity and facility. His furious temper, which sets the *Iliad* moving, is more intense than that of any other warrior, and the fleetness of his foot is that of one who cleaves the air without meeting resistance.[7]

When the Greek forces were gathering for battle, two major warriors did not appear, Odysseus and Achilles. This occurred, according to classicist Barry B. Powell, because Odysseus' wife, Penelope, had recently had a child, Telemachus, and "Odysseus had lost his taste for war."[8] When Agamemnon and Menelaus sent messengers to fetch Odysseus,

> . . . they were astonished to find him on the seashore, dressed like a madman, following a plow to which was hitched a horse and a jackass. Palamedes, son of Nauplius, was not deceived. Famed, like Odysseus, for his cleverness, he had invented the alphabet, dice, numbers, and astronomy. Palamedes seized Telemachus from Penelope's arms, raced to the beach, and cast the child into the sand before the blade of the plow: If Odysseus were mad, he would plow on, but if sane, he would spare his infant son. Odysseus stopped the plow and joined the expeditionary force.[9]

A seer prophesied that Troy could not be captured without Achilles, but that he would die in battle. According to classicists Mark P. O. Morford and Robert J. Lenardon, Achilles' mother, Thetis, tried an unusual method to keep him from serving in the Greek forces:

> To circumvent his early death, she [Thetis] tried to prevent his going by disguising him as a girl and taking him to the island of Scyros, where he was brought up with the daughters of Lycomedes, king of the island. . . . Odysseus and Diomedes exposed Achilles' disguise at Scyros. They took gifts for the daughters of Lycomedes, among them weapons and armor, in which Achilles alone showed any interest. As the women were looking at the gifts, Odysseus arranged for a trumpet to sound; the women all ran away, thinking it was a battle signal, but Achilles took off his disguise and put on the armor.[10]

3

ACHILLES VERSUS HECTOR

INTRODUCTION

The role of fate plays an important part in "Achilles Versus Hector." Achilles knew that his death had been foretold. An oracle, or prophet, prophesied that if Achilles fought at Troy, he would die soon after Hector's death. As such, Achilles' death represents the classic tragedy of the death of each human being. Achilles might strive his hardest, but ultimately, he would die, and he knew it. This attempt by mankind to overcome death became a common theme of many Greek myths.[1]

Another important theme of the myth is the role of the gods. The Olympians interacted with each other and with the human characters. They took sides in the conflict and sometimes even joined in the actual fighting. They tried to affect the outcome of the war by helping a favorite hero or harming one from the opposition. Often, they showed less heroism than the humans for whom they were supposed to set examples.

This story contains two episodes, known as *theomachies*, in which the gods actually fought with each other on the battlefield. Athena and Hera joined with Diomedes, a prince of Argos, in fighting with Aphrodite and Ares. Diomedes wounded Aphrodite, who fled in tears to Mount Olympus. Diomedes also wounded Ares, who received no sympathy about his injuries when he complained to Zeus. In another episode, Hera attacked Artemis, who burst into tears. Thus, the theomachies point out how ridiculous the gods appear when they try to battle like mortals. At the same time, the theomachies demonstrate the difference between human suffering and the minor nature of the divine injuries.[2]

ACHILLES VERSUS HECTOR

The death of his friend Patroclus filled Achilles with deep grief—and feelings of revenge. "The very prophecy that my mother revealed to me has come to pass. She said that the best of my Myrmidons would fall at the hands of Trojans while I was alive. I could not prevent this from happening, even though I warned dear Patroclus not to battle Hector." Achilles rubbed soot and ashes over his face. He rolled in the dirt and tore at his hair and cried out in grief.

His mother, the sea nymph Thetis, heard his cry and swam up from her cave deep in the sea. "Why so sad, my son?" she asked.

"Hector has killed my dear friend, Patroclus. I must return to battle and kill Hector in revenge for slaying my comrade," Achilles said. "Please do not try to hold me back, even though it is fated that my death will follow soon after that of Hector."

In tears, Thetis replied, "You are right, my son, you must save your exhausted comrades from defeat. But your own armor is in the hands of the Trojan prince, Hector. Please wait one more day until you return to battle. I will have Hephaestus, the armorer of the gods, craft you a new set of armor."

Achilles agreed to wait, but was eager to help the Achaeans recover the body of Patroclus with no further delay. Without any armor, Achilles stood before the Trojans and gave a great war cry. The Trojans panicked and retreated. The

Achaeans moved in quickly, retrieved Patroclus' body, and swept from the battlefield.

The Trojans discussed what they should do next. Some wanted to retreat within the safety of the walls of Troy rather than fight out in the open now that Achilles had returned to the battlefield. But Hector had tasted of success in battle. "No more should we hide behind our walls. We have driven the Greeks back to their ships. Surely victory is within our grasp. I will meet Achilles in hand-to-hand combat."

Hector's fellow Trojans roared in agreement at his pronouncement. Little did they know that his advice would prove to be folly.

That night, while Achilles and his men prepared Patroclus' body for a funeral, Thetis flew up to Mount Olympus to get Achilles' new armor. Hephaestus had forged a massive shield, a gleaming breastplate, and a sturdy helmet. After Achilles donned the splendid armor, he went to where the Greek leaders were gathered. "Agamemnon, was it better for both of us and for our comrades that we fought over a slave girl?" he asked. "Instead, let us direct our anger toward our true enemy, the Trojans."

Agamemnon offered Achilles the gifts he had promised him before, but he would not accept blame for his actions. "Achilles, the gods made me act the way I acted. But what is done is done. Let us stop talking and return to battle!"

Achilles answered, "King Agamemnon, do whatever pleases you with these gifts. For now, war calls us."

The next morning, with this mighty warrior leading them, the Greeks stormed onto the battlefield. Achilles fought like a raging lion, slaughtering many Trojans, including Priam's beloved son, Polydorus. As the Trojans fled in Achilles' path, the gates to Troy were flung open, and the Trojan forces sought safety behind their city walls.

Finally, Hector stood alone before the walls of Troy. His parents begged him to come inside the walls, where he would be safe. Yet Hector, as the leader of the Trojans, felt responsible for their losses. He had counseled the Trojans to stay outside the city walls and fight. Hector thought to himself, "It will be more honorable to face Achilles in a duel. Even if I surrender to him, Achilles is filled with such rage that he will kill me anyway."

Yet when Achilles approached Hector, Hector turned and fled, because he saw Athena at Achilles' side. Three times, Hector ran around the city, with Achilles chasing him on foot.

Cunning Athena tricked Hector into stopping by appearing to him in the form of his brother, Deiphobus. Hector thought he could defeat Achilles with the help of his brother. However, Hector did not realize that Athena, in the form of Deiphobus, had disappeared.

Then, Hector asked Achilles to agree to giving the body of whichever one of them died in their fight back to his respective family. "Let us swear to the gods that whoever wins our battle will not mutilate the body of the loser. If I win, once I have stripped your marvelous armor from your body, I will return your corpse to your loyal warriors."

With a dark glance, Achilles refused. "If I win, you will pay for the death of my comrade, Patroclus."

With that, Achilles hurled his spear at Hector. When it missed, Athena brought it back to Achilles. Hector still could not see Athena. After Hector's spear hit the shield of Achilles, he turned to his brother to get another spear. But his brother was not there. Hector realized then that he had been tricked. He vowed not to go to his death without a struggle. He charged toward Achilles, but the Greek drove his spear through Hector's throat.

With his dying breath, Hector begged Achilles to give his body to his father and mother. "Please, allow the Trojans to do me honor once I am dead."

"Do not beg me for mercy, for I plan to feed you to the dogs," Achilles answered.

Hector warned Achilles, "Do not mistreat my body, for the gods will bring their wrath down upon you."

Achilles wrenched his spear from Hector's body and tore the bloody armor off the corpse. The other Greeks ran forward and stabbed the naked body. Then, Achilles pierced Hector's feet and threaded thongs through the holes. He tied the thongs to the back of his chariot and dragged Hector's body around and around the city of Troy. As the Trojans watched from the walls of the city, they were horrified to see the head of their hero dragged behind the chariot.

Achilles and the Myrmidons returned to their camps. They tossed Hector's body face down in the dirt next to the body of Patroclus. Together, thousands of warriors shared a funeral feast. Achilles refused to wash off the blood and dirt that covered his body until he had placed Patroclus on his funeral pyre, or mound of materials piled high for burning a body.

That night, as Achilles slept, Patroclus appeared to him in a dream. "Do not forget me, mighty Achilles," he said. "After you have burned my body, save my ashes in a sacred urn. Make arrangements that when you die, our ashes can be mingled together in one urn."

In the morning, Agamemnon ordered men to cut many trees and pile them into a pyre one hundred feet long and one hundred feet wide and put the body of Patroclus on top of the pyre. Achilles spread fat from slaughtered animal carcasses on the body and arranged the animal skins on top. He set two-handled jars of oil and honey beside Patroclus' body. Achilles then slaughtered twelve Trojans, threw them on the pyre, and set it on fire.

The fire burned for eleven days. All the while, the Achaeans held races and games in honor of Patroclus, as was the custom of the Greeks. They raced chariots, wrestled, and boxed. They feasted day and night. Finally, the ashes and bones of Patroclus were placed in a golden urn, and the urn was placed under a huge mound.

But the gods were furious that although the Greeks had honored Patroclus, they had dishonored Hector. Whenever he wished, Achilles had dragged Hector's body three times around Patroclus' funeral pyre. Zeus summoned Thetis to Mount Olympus. "Go to your son's camp and tell him that the gods are angry with him. We know that in his grief and fury, he still keeps the body of Hector. But it is time for Hector to have a decent burial."

Thetis flew down to warn her son about his behavior. "Achilles, Hector was a man who loved and honored the gods. You have treated him with disrespect. Zeus commands you that it is time to give Hector the hero's burial that he deserves."

Achilles promised, "I will give him back at once to whomever brings a ransom for his body."

At the same time, Zeus sent his messenger, Iris, to Priam of Troy. Iris told Priam to go without fear to Achilles and get his son's body. Hermes, the messenger god, brought Priam safely through the Greek camp by putting the Achaeans to sleep.

When Priam entered Achilles' tent, he begged, "Mighty Achilles, I pray by your honored father and mother to give me back the body of my own dear son." Priam brought to Achilles many rich treasures, such as brocaded robes and bars of gold.

Grief and awe filled Achilles, for Priam reminded Achilles of his own father. Achilles called to his serving women. "Wash Hector's body, and make sure that Priam does not see the terrible wounds on his son's body. Then, dress Hector's body in a finely-woven shirt and wrap it in two soft capes."

When this was done, Achilles gently lifted Hector's body onto a sturdy wagon. He served a fine meal to Priam. The next day, Priam brought his son's body back to the city of Troy. For nine days, the fighting stopped while Hector's family and the people of Troy mourned him. Then, they laid his body on a high funeral pyre and set it afire. When the body had burned away to ashes, the flames were put out with wine. Hector's ashes were collected in a golden chest, which was wrapped in purple cloths. The chest was buried in a hollow grave and covered with huge stones. The Trojans shared a funeral feast in Hector's honor in the house of King Priam of Troy. Thus ended the life of Hector. Next, the fate of Troy would be decided.

QUESTIONS AND ANSWERS

Q: *With Achilles leading the Greeks, what happened in the fighting?*

A: All the Trojans except Hector fled behind their city walls.

Q: *Why did Hector stay outside the walls?*

A: He felt that the Trojan losses were his fault. He knew that he would die at the hands of the Greeks even if he surrendered, so he chose to fight one-on-one with Achilles.

Q: *What did Hector do when Achilles came near him? Why?*

A: Hector fled because he could see Athena at Achilles' side, but he stopped when he thought he saw his brother nearby.

Q: *What did Hector ask Achilles to do? How did Achilles answer?*

A: Hector asked Achilles to agree to give the body of the one who died in their fight back to his family. Achilles refused.

Q: *What dishonorable actions did Achilles perform after defeating Hector?*

A: He stripped the armor off Hector's body, attached the body to the back of his chariot, and dragged it around Troy. He also dragged it around Patroclus' funeral pyre.

Q: *How did Zeus react to Achilles' treatment of Hector's body?*

A: Zeus was furious at this abuse of the dead. He sent Thetis to warn her son to give Hector's body back to Priam. Zeus also sent his messenger, Iris, to Priam to tell him to go without fear to Achilles to ask for his son's body.

Q: *How did Achilles respond to Priam's request?*

A: He was filled with grief and awe at Priam's action. Achilles' servants washed Hector's body, covered it with a fine shirt and soft robes, and gave it to Priam.

EXPERT COMMENTARY

According to classicists Mark P. O. Morford and Robert J. Lenardon, Achilles was a complex main character:

> Again, when the dying Hector foretells Achilles' death, Achilles resolutely accepts his fate. Nor is Achilles always violent. At the funeral games for Patroclus, he presides with princely dignity and even makes peace between the hot-tempered competitors. We have also seen how he gave up his anger against Hector and treated Priam with dignity and generosity. Achilles is a splendid and complex hero, incomparably the greatest figure in the Trojan saga.[3]

An unusual element of the relationship between Achilles and his mother was that they actually met in person several times. According to classicist Robert Fagles:

> Though Achilles and his divine mother Thetis do in fact meet face-to-face (1.422-510, 18.82-162), this is not true of most of the encounters of men and gods in the *Iliad*. Men meet the gods in disguise (in Book 13 Poseidon disguises himself as Calchas) or the god comes to men from behind, as Athena does to Achilles in Book 1 and Apollo to Patroclus in Book 16. In older, legendary times, however, men might entertain the gods in special circumstances; Hera, for example, reminds Apollo (at 24.74-76) that he and all the gods came to the wedding feast for the marriage of Peleus and Thetis.[4]

Hephaestus, the blacksmith, who crafted the shining armor for Achilles, was renowned for his skill as a smith. Fagles noted an unusual characteristic of his:

> Hephaestus, the smith-god, is lame. This may be a reflection of the fact that in a community where agriculture and war are the predominant features in the life of its men, someone with weak legs and strong arms would probably become a blacksmith. He seems to have been lame from birth: at 18.461-64 he says that his mother, Hera, threw him out of Olympus because of this defect. The fall referred to here was probably a consequence of his attempt to help Hera when Zeus had hung her up from Mount Olympus with a pair of anvils tied to her feet.[5]

4

THE TROJAN HORSE

INTRODUCTION

Most of the details about the sack, or destruction, of Troy were recorded in epics which no longer exist. However, in the *Trojan Women* (415 B.C.), Greek dramatist Euripides (480? B.C.–406 B.C.) portrayed Troy's destruction through the eyes of Hecuba, queen of Troy; Cassandra, Trojan prophetess; and Andromache, Hector's widow. The Roman poet Virgil (70 B.C.–19 B.C.) depicted the capture and destruction of Troy in his epic, *Aeneid* (30 B.C.–19 B.C.). The *Aeneid* is considered one of the most important pieces of literature produced in ancient Rome.

The Greeks finally captured the city by trickery, using a plan Odysseus suggested, building a wooden horse to smuggle inside the gates of Troy. The horse is not discussed in the *Iliad*, but many details about it are mentioned in both Book 4 and Book 8 in the *Odyssey*, from which this story is taken. In Book 8, the bard, Demodocus, sings of Odysseus' heroism in planning the creation of the Trojan horse and leading the Greek warriors who were concealed inside. Odysseus himself describes the horse to the ghost of Achilles in the Underworld. He also tells how Achilles' son, Neoptolemus, was the only Greek warrior who waited fearlessly inside the horse. Details about Achilles' death and funeral come from Book 24, where Agamemnon's ghost talks to Achilles' ghost and Thetis mourns her son.

Thetis held funeral games in honor of her deceased son. Such games were a tradition in ancient Greece when a great warrior or nobleman died. Warriors and princes competed against one another in events such as foot races, chariot races, and wrestling.

Ajax, son of Telamon, is an important character in this story. He was always the last of the Greeks to give ground to the Trojans in any battle. He led the fight to recover the body of Patroclus. But even this courage was not enough to win him the honor he expected from his fellow warriors.

THE TROJAN HORSE

Seeking revenge for the death of Patroclus, Achilles charged the Trojan forces and drove them back toward the city gates. Apollo, who supported the Trojans, warned Achilles. "Watch out, Achilles, for although you are a mighty warrior, you are still just a mortal man." Achilles ignored Apollo and fought on with savagery.

Atop the safety of the city walls, Paris sat with his bow and arrows. He drew a single feathered arrow from his quiver, or case for carrying arrows, and inserted it in his bow. When Paris let the arrow fly, Apollo, the god of archery, used his great powers to guide the arrow so that it hit Achilles in his heel. This was the one spot on his body where Achilles was vulnerable. Achilles fell back on top of the bodies of many slain warriors. Soon his eyes, too, misted over in death, and he died, just as was fated. Ajax carried his body from the battlefield while mighty Odysseus held back the Trojans.

The body was placed atop a funeral pyre, and the Greeks shaved their heads to show their sadness. Achilles' mother, Thetis, came up from the sea with her nymphs to mourn Achilles for seventeen days. Many of the Greek heroes paraded around the funeral pyre, adorned in their armor. Achilles' body was anointed with oil and honey. Then on the eighteenth day, the pyre was set ablaze until Achilles' body had burned down to ashes.

Thetis mixed the ashes and bones of Achilles in a golden,

two-handled urn along with those of his friend Patroclus, just as Patroclus had asked. Over the urn, a noble tomb was built, visible from far out at sea. Then, Thetis held funeral games in honor of her dead son.

In the Greek army, the armor of a deceased warrior was given to the mightiest surviving warrior. Both Odysseus and Ajax claimed this prize and spoke before the assembled Achaean armies.

"I claim the honor of receiving the gleaming armor of Achilles," said Odysseus, who was known not only for his strength but also for his powers of persuasion and his craftiness.

Athena, who presided over the assembly, pointed to Ajax to speak next. "No, I am mightier than Odysseus," claimed gigantic Ajax. "Everyone knows that I am second in bravery to Achilles. I am always the last to leave the battlefield."

When Trojan prisoners of war testified that Odysseus had harmed them more than Ajax, Odysseus won the armor. Because he did not earn the prize, Ajax felt disgraced. He thought bitterly, "I am certain that Agamemnon and Menelaus turned the vote against me. They deserve to die, along with Odysseus."

That night, he went to their tents, but Athena caused him to go crazy. He slashed a flock of sheep with his sword, believing the creatures to be the Greek army. He beat to death a huge ram, thinking it was Odysseus. Then, he suddenly came to his senses and realized what he had done. In horror and shame, Ajax fell on his own sword and killed himself.

In a short span of time, the Greeks had lost two great heroes, Achilles and Ajax. It seemed that they would never win the war. A prophet then told the Greeks that they needed Neoptolemus, the son of Achilles, to join the fighting. The Palladium, a sacred statue of Athena, had to be captured from within Troy. The Greeks also needed to use the bow and arrow of the long-deceased hero, Heracles, in battle.

Odysseus and Diomedes convinced Neoptolemus to join

the Greek forces. Odysseus and Diomedes also climbed over the walls of Troy in the dark of night and stole the Palladium. The archer, Philoctetes, had the bow and arrows of Heracles. The spirit of Heracles convinced Philoctetes to join the Greeks. Neoptolemus and Philoctetes proved to be able warriors. Neoptolemus fought with great bravery and savagery. Philoctetes, whose aim was true, fired the arrow of Heracles' that killed Paris.

Yet despite the death of Paris, the Achaeans still could not win Troy. In ten years of fighting, the city walls had not been damaged. The Greeks finally realized that they could never conquer Troy unless they could get their armed forces inside the city.

Odysseus proposed a clever idea, which the Greeks decided to try. They built a gigantic wooden horse with a trap door in its belly. Led by Odysseus, fifty of the boldest Greek warriors climbed inside. Among them were Diomedes, Menelaus, and Neoptolemus. The remainder of the Greeks burned their tents and moved back on board ship. The ships pretended to sail for home, but actually they hid just out of sight of the Trojan forces. The giant horse was left outside the city walls.

The Trojans could not believe their eyes when they saw the horse. It was so enormous that it was terrifying. Just as amazing was the sight of the empty Greek camp and the absence of the Greek ships. Surely this meant that the Greeks had given up and gone home.

For many days, the Trojans sat around the horse and debated what to do with it. They were divided among three plans.

"I think we should hack open the belly of the horse with mighty bronze weapons," said one warrior. Others nodded in agreement.

"No, we should drag it to the edge of the highest ridge and throw it down the cliffs," said others.

"The safest plan would be to leave it standing as an

offering to the gods," said other warriors. "How can we fail to succeed if we honor the gods?"

This was the choice the Trojans made. Unfortunately, it was fated that the city of Troy would be destroyed once they possessed the wooden horse.

Outside the city walls, the Trojans also discovered a Greek named Sinon, who pretended to be a bitter enemy of Odysseus that the Greeks had left behind at Troy. He told them a story that Odysseus had made up to trick the Trojans.

"The Greeks made Athena very angry when they stole her Palladium from Troy," said Sinon. "She demanded a blood sacrifice, and I was chosen to be the victim. The Greeks believed that such a sacrifice would bring them a safe journey home."

"Why are you still alive?" asked a Trojan warrior.

"The night before I was to be sacrificed, I escaped," Sinon answered. "I hid in a swamp, watching until all the ships had sailed away."

"What, then, is the purpose of this massive horse?" asked another warrior.

"The Greeks believed that Athena turned against them," Sinon said. "They created the horse as a sacrifice to win her favor."

"But why is it so large?" asked another Trojan.

"The wily Greeks do not wish you to take it within your walls," Sinon explained. "If you do, the city will never be captured. But if it is left outside, the Greeks will one day return and totally destroy Troy."

Crafty Odysseus had truly created a good tale, for few of the Trojans doubted Sinon's story. Still, the prophetess Cassandra, Priam's daughter, warned against bringing the horse within the walls. "Beware, Trojans, for this mighty horse will bring disaster to our city. Your wives will become slaves to the Greeks. Your children will perish. Your riches will be taken by the Greeks, who will show you no mercy at all."

Unfortunately, no one ever believed Cassandra. She had once agreed to make love with Apollo, but then changed her mind. Apollo punished her by making it so that Cassandra's predictions would never be believed.

Laocoön, a Trojan priest, threw his spear against the horse's flanks. Laocoön insisted, "Do not bring the horse inside the city walls. Danger lurks inside its belly. The horse should be destroyed." Soon after Laocoön said this, two huge serpents came up from the sea and strangled the priest and his two young sons, who screamed in terror.

"Surely this is a sign sent by the gods," said the Trojans, who watched in horror. "Anyone who opposes bringing the horse inside the city walls will be punished."

With ropes made of flax, the Trojans dragged the horse through the city gates to the temple of Athena and offered it to the goddess with thanks. That night, the Trojans celebrated what they thought was their victory over the Greeks. Young women danced to the music of flutes. But in reality, they had brought death into their city.

The hiding place of the Greeks might even then have been uncovered. Helen walked around the horse, calling various Greek warriors by name. She imitated the voice of each man's wife. But Odysseus kept any of the Greeks from answering.

Meanwhile, that night as the Trojans slept, Sinon signalled to the fleet of Greek ships, which sailed silently back to Troy. He also opened the horse to release the warriors hidden inside. Soon the reunited Greek forces had set the city of Troy ablaze.

The Trojans awoke in confusion to blood-curdling war cries. Chariots thundered down the dusty streets. When the Trojans rushed out into the streets, they were struck down by waiting bands of Greek warriors, clad in fearsome armor and spiked helmets. The Achaeans slashed at the Trojans with sharp spears. They slaughtered their women and children or took them prisoner. Rivers of blood flowed in the streets.

Even Priam, the king, was not safe. After Greek warriors broke down the doors of the palace, Neoptolemus stabbed

Priam at the altar of Zeus, just as Neoptolemus' father, Achilles, had killed Hector, Priam's son.

Menelaus found Helen in the home of her new husband, Deiphobus, a son of Priam whom Helen had married soon after the death of Paris. Menelaus slaughtered Deiphobus and was about to kill Helen when she pleaded with him to save her life. When the Greek fleet sailed, Menelaus took Helen with him, and they lived together happily for many years.

But the lives of the other Trojan women were fated to be unhappy. The Greeks grouped them together outside the ruins of the city. Each warrior received at least one of the women as a slave. Hector's wife, Andromache, became the slave of Neoptolemus. Astyanax, the son of Hector, was torn from his mother's arms and thrown from the city walls. Hector's mother, Hecuba, became a slave to Odysseus. Polyxena, Priam's youngest daughter, was sacrificed over the tomb of Achilles. As their city perished, the surviving women of Troy, victims of war, waited for the Greek ships to take them away to slavery.

QUESTIONS AND ANSWERS

Q: *How did Achilles die?*

A: Paris shot an arrow at Achilles. Apollo guided the arrow so that it hit Achilles in his heel, the only spot on his body that was vulnerable.

Q: *Describe Achilles' funeral.*

A: First, his body was placed atop a funeral pyre and set on fire. His ashes were mixed with those of his friend Patroclus. They were placed in a golden urn and buried in a giant tomb. Then, Thetis held funeral games in honor of her dead son.

Q: *What happened to Achilles' armor? Why?*

A: Greek custom awarded the armor of a deceased warrior to the leading surviving warrior. Both Ajax and Odysseus claimed this honor. The Greeks voted to give the armor to Odysseus, because Trojan war prisoners testified that Odysseus was the better warrior.

Q: *What did a prophet tell the Greeks that they needed to do to win the war?*

A: They needed to get Neoptolemus to join the fighting, use the bow and arrows of the hero Heracles, and capture the Palladium.

Q: *What idea did Odysseus propose to win the war?*

A: He suggested that the Greeks build a gigantic wooden horse and hide some of the Greek army inside. Then, they should burn their tents and have their ships sail just out of sight of Troy. This would look like they had left the battlefield.

Q: *How were the Trojans convinced to take the horse inside their city walls?*

A: The Greeks left behind a warrior named Sinon, who told a clever story that Odysseus had invented. Sinon said that the Greeks had angered Athena by stealing her Palladium. He was chosen to be the sacrifice which would appease Athena, but he hid before the Greeks could put him to death. Sinon said that if the horse was left outside the city walls, the Greeks would return to destroy Troy someday.

Q: *Did all the Trojans believe Sinon?*

A: No, the prophetess Cassandra and the priest Laocoön warned against bringing the horse inside the walls.

Q: *What happened to Laocoön? What did the Trojans think this meant?*

A: After he gave his warning, two serpents came out of the sea and strangled Laocoön and his two sons. The Trojans took this as a sign that anyone who opposed bringing the horse inside the walls would die.

Q: *What happened during the night after the Trojans brought the horse inside the walls?*

A: Sinon signaled to the Greek ships to return to Troy. He also let the warriors out of the horse's belly. The Greeks then attacked the sleeping Trojans and destroyed their city.

EXPERT COMMENTARY

Robert Graves, a historical novelist, noted that the horse was the sacred animal of Troy. Yet classical writers on Homer felt that a device other than an actual wooden horse might have been used to break down the walls of Troy. The Greeks might have entered:

> . . . into Troy by a postern (gate) which had a horse painted on it; or that the sign of a horse was used to distinguish the Greeks from their enemies in the darkness and confusion; or that when Troy had been betrayed, the oracles forbade the plundering of any house marked with the sign of a horse . . .; or that Troy fell as a result of a cavalry action; or that the Greeks, after burning their camp, concealed themselves behind Mount Hippius ("of the horse.")[1]

The myths about the Trojan horse provided inspiration to ancient Greek art. Professor Barry B. Powell described a large jar or vase from about 670 B.C. as:

> . . . one of the earliest surviving unequivocal references to myth in Greek art. The horse is on wheels and has openings through which we can see the heads of the heroes. From the portholes swords and shields are passed out. Some heroes have already come down and are striding off in full armor to the battle. Other scenes on the jar portray scenes of mayhem, the death of children and the rape of women.[2]

A modern expression has its roots in the story of the Trojan Horse, according to Powell:

> A priest of Poseidon, Laocoön, also suspected that the horse held warriors. He came forward and declared Sinon, like all Greeks, to be a liar (hence the saying, "beware Greeks bearing gifts").[3]

5

THE
LOTUS-EATERS

INTRODUCTION

After their victory in the Trojan War, Odysseus and the rest of the Greek army set out for their homes. The journey of Odysseus is depicted in Homer's epic, the *Odyssey*. The word *odyssey* has come to mean a journey or quest, specifically "a long wandering or voyage usually marked by many changes of fortune."[1] The Greek word *odusseia* means "the story of Odysseus."[2] Odysseus' wandering voyage home took ten years and was filled with adventures and changes of fortune.

The journeys of the Greek leaders other than Odysseus were described in an epic entitled *Nostoi* (meaning "Returns" or "Homecoming"), which is now lost. Only a brief summary of this poem exists and does not mention Odysseus. Nostoi is the root of our word nostalgia, or homesickness.

The *Odyssey*, like the *Iliad*, was written in the late eighth century B.C. Historians feel that it was composed after the *Iliad*, because Homer assumed that the reader of the *Odyssey* had knowledge of the Trojan War. Also, he did not duplicate events described in the *Iliad*.

Odysseus was the most admired of the Greek heroes. He thought before he acted. He was clever and crafty, as shown by his idea of the Trojan horse. His use of disguises played a crucial part in the *Odyssey*. In contrast, Achilles displayed a fiery temper and a tendency to act first before carefully thinking through his options.

A key theme of the *Odyssey* is that of a fantastic journey. Still, the epic portrays more than just exciting adventures. Odysseus faced challenges throughout his journey. Women that he met tempted him to stay with them and abandon his wife, Penelope. Also, Odysseus had to fight against the lure of staying where life was easy and luxurious. If he had given in to the lure of luxury, he never would have completed his journey home to his wife and family. Thus, his odyssey became a journey of personal growth.

In this epic, Homer drew a parallel between the *Odyssey*

and all of life. Humans face challenges throughout their lifetimes. Evil and good exist alongside of each other. People can make mistakes and yet be forgiven. They can learn from their errors. Hence, the Odyssey is not just a myth of entertainment. It is an epic for education.

The *Odyssey* particularly influenced Irish writer James Joyce (1882–1941). In several handwritten notebooks, Joyce patterned his novel *Ulysses* after the *Odyssey*. He created several characters who parallel those of Homer's epic. He also used similar themes, such as a son's search for his father and the interference of the gods in the lives of the characters. His novel, however, is set in Ireland in the early 1900s.

In the *Odyssey*, Odysseus retold his adventures at a banquet at the court of King Alcinoüs, ruler of the kindly Phaeacians. Odysseus had washed ashore on their island. One of the first tales Odysseus told the Phaeacians was about the Lotus-Eaters.

THE LOTUS-EATERS

After the Greeks won the Trojan War, they celebrated wildly. Unfortunately, they forgot that the gods expected honor and praise for their part in the victory. As the Greeks celebrated, they dragged Cassandra, a priestess of Athena, out of her temple. Athena was furious at the disrespect the Greeks showed to her priestess. She convinced Poseidon to cause terrible storms to destroy the Greek ships as they sailed for home. Agamemnon lost almost all of his ships, while storms forced Menelaus all the way to Egypt.

Odysseus did not die, but his voyage was long and dangerous. Before he left for Troy, Odysseus had known that it would be twenty years before he would return home to the island of Ithaca. The war would last ten years, while his return voyage would take another ten years. At times, Odysseus wondered whether he would ever see his wife, Penelope, and his son, Telemachus, again.

Odysseus and the crewmen of his twelve ships started their voyage home, but they hoped to capture more treasure on the way. Then without warning, Zeus, who commanded the storm clouds, hit the ships with a howling gale that tore the sails to rags. Mightily, the sailors rowed to the nearest shoreline, where they rested for two days and two nights. But when the ships set out anew, the raging winds blew again for nine more days. The winds drove the ships far off course to an unknown, foreign land. The sailors beached the ships and charged ashore, desperate for food and water.

"Eat and drink now, men, for we do not know what we shall face in this land," said Odysseus. Always curious, Odysseus sent three men ahead to scout out their surroundings. "Search out this land and find out who might live here. When you have learned any helpful information, one of you should come back and report to me."

The scouts soon came to a small hut where they found several men lounging around a basket of fragrant fruit. "Greetings, sailors, welcome to the land of the Lotus-Eaters. Try some of our lotus," said one of the men, with a friendly, dreamy smile.

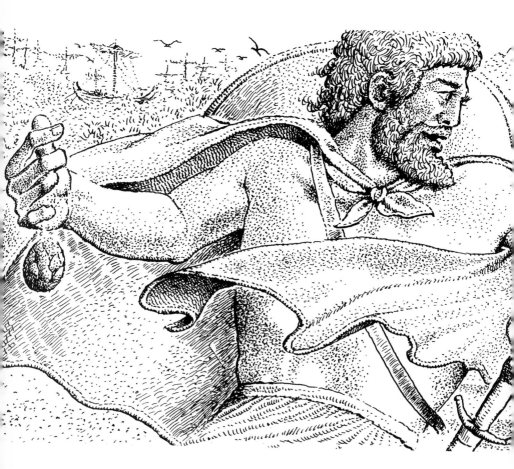

"I have never seen fruit like this," said one of the sailors. "What does it taste like?"

"It is sweet like honey," answered the Lotus-Eaters. "There is nothing like it anywhere."

At first, the sailors took small bites, but they were hungry after sailing for so many days in stormy weather. Soon, they snatched at every lotus fruit they could reach. Honey-sweet juices flowed down their chins. As the men ate, they fell in love with the land of the Lotus-Eaters, for whoever ate a lotus lost all memory of his past life and never wanted to return home again.

After several hours, Odysseus realized that something was wrong. Fearing that his soldiers might have been killed,

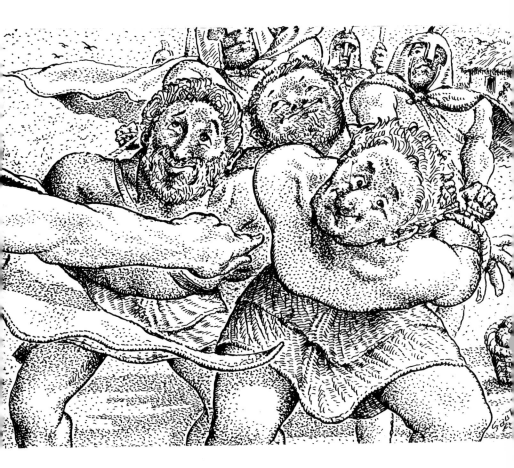

he gathered a search party. Quickly, the search party set off through the woods. They soon found their comrades, eating lotus and smiling dreamy smiles. One of the happy sailors handed a fruit to Odysseus. "Try a lotus. They are the most wonderful fruit on earth!"

Odysseus refused the fruit. "Come, men," he said. "It is time to resume our journey to our home and our families."

The three sailors looked confused. "Home? Families? Who would want to live anywhere other than this island?"

Odysseus wondered what had caused his sailors' forgetfulness. He reached down and picked up one of the lotus fruits. As soon as he sniffed it, he immediately felt a wave of forgetfulness. Fearing that he, too, would lose all desire to journey home, Odysseus quickly dropped the lotus fruit. "Tie up these three men," Odysseus commanded his search party. "Make haste to return to our ships. We cannot take a chance on any more of our crew eating the lotus fruit."

The search party grabbed hold of the scouting party, and the three scouts began to weep. They were having such a wonderful time eating the lotus that they had no desire at all to return to their ships.

"Haul them to the rowing benches," Odysseus ordered his search party. "Lash them fast so that they cannot escape."

All the remaining sailors jumped aboard at once. They grabbed their oars and churned up the water to white foam with stroke after stroke of the oars.

"Quickly, men, we have no time to lose!" Odysseus urged them on. "That's the way. We must make haste to leave the land of the Lotus-Eaters far behind us."

Little did Odysseus know that another adventure awaited him.

QUESTIONS AND ANSWERS

Q: What did the Greeks do after winning the Trojan War?

A: They celebrated wildly, dragging Cassandra, a priestess of Athena, out of Athena's temple.

Q: How did Athena punish the Greeks for their treatment of Cassandra?

A: She convinced Poseidon to cause terrible storms that destroyed or knocked off course the ships of the Greeks.

Q: How long was Odysseus gone from his home?

A: He fought in the Trojan War for ten years and his journey home took another ten years.

Q: When Odysseus and his crewmen started their voyage home, what did Zeus do?

A: He caused winds to blow them off course.

Q: What did Odysseus do when he and his men first landed on the island of the Lotus-Eaters?

A: He sent out a scouting party of three men.

Q: What happened to these men?

A: They ate the lotus fruit, which made them lose memory of their past lives and instead want to remain on the island.

Q: What did Odysseus do when his scouting party did not return?

A: He and a search party found them, sitting and eating lotus. Odysseus and his search party dragged the missing men back to the ships.

Q: How did the scouting party react when they could no longer eat the lotus?

A: They wept, because they had no desire to return to their ships.

EXPERT COMMENTARY

According to Professor Barry B. Powell:

> The figure of Odysseus, the Roman Ulysses, has always fascinated the imagination of the West. Although many meanings have been given to him, he is always cast in one of two categories: either glorified as the seeker of truth, the restless clever intelligence penetrating the secrets of the world, or damned as the treacherous deceiver, the exalter of intellect above the demands of the heart. Homer's Odysseus belongs to the first category, but the anti-Odysseus tradition appears as early as Sophocles' *Philoctetes* (409 B.C.) and is then refined by Euripides, Virgil, and others.[3]

Powell noted that the Romans held a particularly negative view of Odysseus:

> The Romans especially developed the tradition hostile to Odysseus because they claimed Aeneas, a Trojan, as their founder. In his *Divine Comedy*, Dante Alighieri (1265–1321) follows this tradition, for he saw legitimate political power in his own world as descending from the Roman state. Dante's is the first important portrayal of Odysseus in a nonclassical language.[4]

The positive viewpoint of Odysseus did not resurface until the nineteenth century:

> The pro-Odysseus tradition reappears in *Ulysses* of Alfred, Lord Tennyson (1809–1902), the most famous English poet of the Victorian age, who glorifies the very qualities Dante condemns. The poem is set on Ithaca. Ulysses has grown old, but is determined to leave home again in pursuit of fresh adventure. . . .[5]

To Homer and the Greeks, Odysseus was a real character in a real world. An important part of both of Homer's epics is plot and character:

> Homer realized the need for a plot in a story describing a struggle that has a beginning, middle, and end. As far as we know, the device of a plot was Homer's invention: subsequent

long poems, drama, novels, and feature films are indebted to him. . . . Homer is also the inventor of character ("imprint") in literature, although his methods of portraying character are different from a modern novelist's. He never describes to us the inner life of his characters, but places them directly in the midst of events where they speak and act. He gives the sense that we are witnessing the lives of real men and women living in a real, though stylized, world.[6]

6

THE CYCLOPS

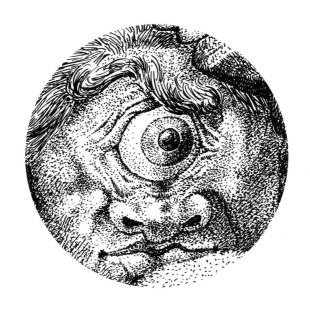

INTRODUCTION

After leaving the land of the Lotus-Eaters, Odysseus and his men set out to sea again. They came to an island where the Cyclops named Polyphemus lived. Cyclops means "round-eye" and refers to the terrible single eye that the monster had in the center of his forehead. Polyphemus, whose name means "much-renowned," was the son of Poseidon, the god of the sea. Polyphemus was a simple shepherd who lived in a dark cave with his sheep. He and the other Cyclopes who lived on the island did not have any form of organized government, nor were they intelligent.

Polyphemus represented one of Odysseus' worst enemies. He stood for everything that the Achaean civilization despised. He showed no respect for the gods and was not hospitable to strangers. In fact, he ate human flesh. He drank too much wine. He did not even get along with his fellow Cyclopes. Polyphemus symbolized the savagery that can take over all men who do not live in a civilized society.

Gigantic creatures like Polyphemus are commonly found in mythology. The Norse frost giant Ymir is such a monster. Because of their sheer size, these creatures are frightening. But they are often portrayed as stupid and easy to outwit, as was Polyphemus.

Legend has it that the cave of Polyphemus is in eastern Sicily, where there are seven rocks called the "Scogli de Cyclopi" in Italian.[1] They represent the rocks which Polyphemus threw at Odysseus after the hero escaped in his ship.

An important theme of the *Odyssey* is Odysseus' victory over death, which threatened him on so many occasions. In this story, Polyphemus' cave represented darkness and death.[2] The number of men in his crew, twelve sailors and himself, totalled the unlucky number thirteen. Water also presented a threat of death in the person of the sea god, Poseidon, who sought revenge against Odysseus for his treatment of Polyphemus.

THE CYCLOPS

After the adventure in the land of the Lotus-Eaters, Odysseus unknowingly sailed his ships to an island where an even more terrible fate awaited his sailors. Odysseus went ashore with a dozen of his finest fighters, carrying a skin full of wine. He left the rest of the crew to guard his ship.

Odysseus soon discovered a cave with a gigantic stone rolled to one side of the entrance. "Come, comrades, let us explore this cavern. Perhaps we will find rich treasure hidden inside."

Quickly, the men strode through the rough entrance. Large, flat racks stored stacks of cheeses. Pails brimming with sheep's milk stood nearby. Lambs bleated in their corrals.

"Well, I had in mind treasures of gold and jewels to fill our ships. But treasures of rich food will stand us well on our journey," said Odysseus. He and his men offered the best of the cheeses in thanks to the gods, and then began to eat.

Just then, in stomped the shepherd who owned the cave, herding his sheep before him. High overhead, he hoisted a massive slab of rock and wedged it in front of the door to his cave. This was no ordinary shepherd—it was the Cyclops Polyphemus, a gigantic one-eyed monster, son of Poseidon, god of the sea. Polyphemus was terrible to look at, with straggling hair, a wild beard, and a single, bulging eye.

"Strangers!" the monster roared. "Where have you sailed from? Why do you steal my food?"

Even mighty Odysseus found himself trembling in fear at the sight of the monster, but he gathered courage and answered. "We are men of Achaea, bound for home after our victory at Troy. Warring winds drove us far off course. Please welcome us as guests, as Zeus commands."

"You must think me a fool," retorted Polyphemus. "I never trouble myself over what the gods want. I have no fear of Zeus." Then he reached down and grabbed two of Odysseus' men and swallowed them. After a few bites, he washed down his feast with some sheep's milk. Giving a mighty yawn, Polyphemus staggered over to the corner of the cave, wrapped himself in a sheepskin blanket, and fell asleep.

Odysseus whispered to his remaining men, "I am tempted to stab the creature in the heart with my sword. But if I do, we will be trapped in this cave. Although we are strong, we cannot roll away the vast stone from the door."

When morning came, the Cyclops ate two more of Odysseus' men. Then, he drove his sheep out of the cave and easily slipped the gigantic doorslab back in place.

As soon as the Cyclops was gone, Odysseus revealed a clever plan to escape the monster. Odysseus found the giant's olivewood club lying beside the sheep pens. He chopped off a length and sharpened the tip to a stabbing point. He charred the point in the fire to make sure that it was hard. Then, he hid the stick and awaited the monster's return.

With a mighty thump, the stone was rolled away from the cave's doorway. "Where are those tasty morsels of men?" said the Cyclops, looking from side to side with his terrible eye. Odysseus' men tried to hide, but Polyphemus reached down and grabbed two more sailors.

Odysseus found a wooden bowl in the depths of the cave, and filled it with wine that he had brought from his ship. "Please accept my gift and think kindly of us, for we are at your mercy. This is wine, a drink as sweet as ambrosia, the food of the gods. It tastes far better than sheep's milk," said Odysseus.

The monster seized the bowl of wine and swallowed

every last drop. Odysseus poured him three more bowls, and he drank them down. The Cyclops had never before sampled wine, and he soon became drunk. "Yes, I will offer you a guest gift," he burped. "What is your name?"

Odysseus answered, "My name is Nobody."

"Well, Nobody," laughed Polyphemus, "my gift to you is that I will eat you last." With that, he fell over backward in a drunken sleep.

Quickly, Odysseus and his men carried their sharpened stick over to the giant's fire and stuck the pointed end into the flames. Then they plunged the red-hot stick into the monster's terrible single eye, twisting and turning it, back and forth, until they blinded the Cyclops.

The monster let loose a terrible roar that echoed off the cavern walls. He yanked the stick from his eye and blood gushed out. Crying out in pain, he tossed the stick aside. He called to his neighboring Cyclopes for help.

"What is the matter, Polyphemus?" they asked. "You have awakened all of us in the middle of the night. Who is bothering you?"

"Nobody is trying to kill me," answered Polyphemus.

"If you are by yourself and nobody is trying to harm you, then Zeus must have sent a deadly disease to plague you," said the Cyclopes. "You should pray to your father, Poseidon, for help." With that, the other Cyclopes lumbered off.

Then, Odysseus told his remaining men of a plan that would save them from the monster. "In the morning, before Polyphemus lets his sheep out to graze, we will tie ourselves under the bellies of the sheep. With his blinded eye, the Cyclops will not be able to see us."

When the new day dawned, Polyphemus opened his cave door to allow his sheep out to pasture. As the animals went out the cave door, the blinded Cyclops felt around for the men who had caused him such a terrible injury. But all he could feel were the backs of the sheep.

When the sheep reached the meadows where they grazed, Odysseus and his men let go of the wooly animals.

They dashed to their boat, taking some of the sheep with them. With everyone safely on board, the ship quickly put out to sea. Odysseus called out in a loud voice, "It was no weak coward you had trapped in your cave. It was I, Odysseus, who tricked you, Polyphemus!"

Rage boiled over inside the Cyclops. He tore off the top of a mountain and heaved it so hard that it landed in front of Odysseus' ship. A huge wave arose and nearly knocked Odysseus and his men off their boat. But the sailors rowed hard, and the ship escaped.

Polyphemus was so furious that he bellowed out to his father, Poseidon. "Hear me, father, lord of the seas. Grant that Odysseus will never reach home. Or at least make it that he arrives home late, a broken man. Let him find a world of pain at home."

The god of the sea honored the prayer of Polyphemus, promising that Odysseus would not reach his home in Ithaca again for ten years and that he would lose all of his men on his journey.

QUESTIONS AND ANSWERS

Q: *Describe Polyphemus.*

A: He was a gigantic, one-eyed monster with straggling hair and a wild beard.

Q: *To which god was Polyphemus related?*

A: His father was Poseidon, god of the sea.

Q: *When Polyphemus found Odysseus and his men inside his cave, what did he do?*

A: He ate two of the men and rolled a large stone in front of the cave's door, trapping Odysseus and the rest of his crew inside.

Q: *When Polyphemus asked Odysseus his name, what did the hero say?*

A: He said, "My name is Nobody."

Q: *Describe how Odysseus attacked the Cyclops.*

A: He offered Polyphemus wine that made him fall into a drunken sleep. Then Odysseus and his men blinded Polyphemus by stabbing the monster in the eye with the sharpened stick he had made.

Q: *Who did Polyphemus tell the other Cyclopes was trying to kill him and how did they react?*

A: He said that "nobody" was trying to kill him. The other Cyclopes said, "If nobody is trying to harm you, then Zeus must have sent a deadly disease to plague you." The Cyclopes told Polyphemus to pray to Poseidon for help.

Q: *How did Polyphemus strike back at Odysseus after he escaped?*

A: He tore off a mountaintop and threw it at Odysseus' ship.

Q: *How did Poseidon grant his son's request?*

A: He promised to delay Odysseus' return home.

EXPERT COMMENTARY

According to Professor Barry B. Powell, Homer gives the ancient Greek custom of *xenia*, the hospitality shown to guests, a new twist in this story: "The gift of Cyclops parodies, by inversion, the custom of *xenia*—Odysseus will be eaten last!"[3]

The tool that Odysseus used to blind the Cyclops, according to Powell:

> . . . is like a bow drill, whose forward thrust comes from the weight of the user as he leans against it. The twist of the drill came from a long thong wrapped in a single turn around it: men at each end pushed and pulled so it turned, now clockwise, now counterclockwise, like the drill of someone starting a fire by friction. But the simile is somewhat mixed: How could Odysseus both guide the stake and twist it, especially if its weight was being carried by four other men?[4]

Polyphemus learned from a prophecy that Odysseus would visit him:

> A seer named Telemus had once warned Polyphemus that a man named Odysseus would blind him. But Polyphemus was too heartbroken to pay attention to this oracle. The grotesque Cyclops had loved the sea nymph Galatea, but she only had eyes for the handsome human youth Acis. Polyphemus had crushed his rival under a giant rock. But Galatea only hated him more after this murder, while Acis—in answer to her prayers—was changed into a river god.[5]

According to scholar and historian Michael Grant:

> Odysseus resembles the typical hero of the *Iliad* in his unconquerable, enduring great heart. By this he survives fantastic obstacles. . . . He overcomes them by the sheer force of his character, amazingly resourceful, yet recklessly ferocious. He is the type, for all time, of a man who has battled with the varied storms of life and won. Miraculous though his adventures are, yet they illuminate his character and confirm his violent belief, like Ivan Karamazov's, in his own powers.[6]

However, even though Odysseus resembled the typical hero of the *Iliad*, Grant noted that he exhibited one characteristic difference, which he demonstrated in his dealings with Polyphemus:

> Yet there is one exceptional feature about this heavy-jawed, beetle-browed hero. He is tremendously clever, far more clever than any hero of the Iliad. In his heroic character an unexpectedly prominent, indeed pre-eminent, part is played by intelligence, assuming multifarious forms from strategic and tactical sageness to the weaving of an endless web of lies and fancies.[7]

Writers of the classical period in Greek history, according to Grant, held negative opinions of Odysseus' cleverness:

> The classical fifth century usually, though not always, regarded Odysseus as an evil product of overcleverness: cruel, corrupt, sophistical and deceitful, a hardboiled confidence man. "May I never," said the old-fashioned, aristocratic Pindar, "have a character like that, but walk in straightforward ways." To Sophocles, Odysseus is a magnanimous hero in the *Ajax*, but a cold blooded schemer in the *Philoctetes*. So he is in several plays of Euripides, written in the age of the Peloponnesian War, when many people thought that cleverness was ruining Athens.[8]

7

CIRCE,
THE BEWITCHING
QUEEN

INTRODUCTION

After Odysseus and his men escaped from the Cyclops Polyphemus, they sailed to the island of Aeolus, King of the Winds. Aeolus lived on the island with his six sons, who were married to his six daughters. He was known for his hospitality, but as we shall see in the story, Odysseus' men abused this hospitality, with disastrous results for the crew. Ultimately, Odysseus ended up on the island of Aeaea, home of the sorceress Circe.

Circe was the daughter of the Sun and Perse, a nymph. Her brother, Aeëtes, was the father of Medea, another sorceress. Although Circe used a wand, she did not resemble a witch as we usually think of one. She did not wear a black hat and robe or have a wart on her nose. Instead, Homer called her "The Bewitching Queen of Aeaea."[1] She wore her hair in long braids and sang with a melodious voice.

Her island has been identified with the island of Ischia in the Bay of Naples.[2] In about 800 B.C., Greeks from the island of Euboea, east of Attica, sailed in small open boats all the way to Italy, where they settled the first Greek colonies. The *Odyssey*, according to some experts, may have been written down on Euboea at about this time, and those who listened to the tales, especially the Greek seafarers, associated the adventures of Odysseus with specific geographic locations around Italy.[3]

This story uses a device similar to one used in the story about the Lotus-Eaters, a food that produces the loss of memory. However, in this case, the loss of memory is caused by a magical potion that Circe made.

In this tale, Hermes, Zeus' messenger, gives Odysseus a protective herb. It was the magic herb *moly*, whose "root is black and flower as white as milk."[4] Moly served as an antidote, to counteract the effects of Circe's magical drugs.

CIRCE, THE BEWITCHING QUEEN

Zeus had given Aeolus, the King of the Winds, the power to rouse the winds or to calm them. When Aeolus heard of the struggles of Odysseus and his sailors to reach home, he decided to help them. In keeping with the custom of hospitality, Aeolus gave Odysseus a special gift, a leather bag that contained all the strongest, most dangerous winds. Aeolus cautioned Odysseus not to open the bag if he wanted to reach home safely.

Unfortunately, some of the crew thought King Aeolus had given Odysseus a sack full of gold, which he was unwilling to share with them. One day, when the ship was nearly home, Odysseus took a nap. This was the opportunity for which his men had been waiting. They opened the bag, but there was no gold inside. Only fierce winds rushed out.

The winds pushed the ships to the land of the Laestrygonians, a race of gigantic cannibals. These creatures used rocks to smash all of Odysseus' fleet, except for his ship, which was anchored in a different place. They also ate up all Odysseus' men except for those manning his vessel.

Odysseus' tired and discouraged crew put back out to sea and eventually came to the island of Aeaea, the land of Circe, the sorceress. She had been expecting Odysseus or someone like him, because a prophecy foretold that a heroic man would someday defy her magic.

Odysseus sent out a search party led by his trusted and

brave warrior, Eurylochus. Deep in the woods, they came to a palace. Built of magnificent stone, it rose high above the forest. Mountain lions and wolves roamed the grounds. These beasts approached Odysseus' men, who backed away, fearful that the animals would attack. But the creatures only pawed at the ground and swished their long tails.

Just then, the men heard unearthly singing coming from inside the palace. One of the warriors peered inside. "I can see a lovely woman with long braids working at her loom."

After the men called out to her, the woman opened the gleaming palace doors. "Welcome! I am Circe. Please, come inside."

All the men rushed in except for Eurylochus, who sensed a trap. Circe invited them to sit on high-backed chairs. In drinking bowls, she mixed a fragrant brew of cheese, barley, honey, and wine. But the men did not see her stir in drugs. These drugs would erase their memories of home.

Once the sailors had drained their bowls of potion, Circe drew out her witch's wand, touched the men, and transformed all of them, except Eurylochus, into pigs. She herded them, squealing and crying, into pigpens. But they kept their human brains, so they were aware of the terrible fate which had befallen them.

Eurylochus ran back to the ship in panic to tell Odysseus what had happened to the rest of the crew. He could hardly speak, because he was so horrified by the disaster.

Odysseus grabbed his bronze sword and slung his bow and arrows over his shoulder. "Lead me back the same way you came, Eurylochus."

"No, captain, let us escape while we can. You will never bring any of those men back alive," Eurylochus answered.

Odysseus told Eurylochus to stay behind at the ship, and set out alone to rescue his men. On the way, he met Hermes, who gave him an herb that would protect him from Circe's charms.

"Take this herb, Odysseus. Without it, you will be trapped here, just like the rest of your men," warned Hermes. "My

herb will protect you from Circe's drugged wine. Then, when she brings out her wand, draw your sword and rush at her as if you are going to stab her. She will be so frightened that she will try to convince you to fall in love with her. Make her promise that she will release your crew and not do you any harm."

Odysseus approached the palace and shouted out to Circe. At once, she opened the gleaming palace doors and welcomed him inside. She led Odysseus to an ornately carved chair and mixed her potion in a golden bowl, stirring in her poison. But because of Hermes' magic herb, Odysseus did not fall prey to the poison.

"Who are you?" cried Circe in astonishment. "No other man has ever withstood my potion."

"I am mighty Odysseus, one of the Achaean warriors who won the Trojan War. Now you must turn those pigs back into my men."

When Odysseus was reunited with this crew, Circe treated them all to a sumptuous feast. She was such a wonderful hostess that they ended up staying with her for an entire year.

But finally, Odysseus' men reminded him of their need to return home to Ithaca. Circe told Odysseus what he had to do to safely reach Ithaca. First, he had to cross the River Ocean and sail beyond the western edge of the world to visit with the prophet Tiresias in the Underworld. There, he would have to sacrifice a ram and some sheep and fill a pit with their blood to attract the ghosts in the Underworld, all of whom craved blood.

Odysseus did as Circe instructed him. When Tiresias appeared, Odysseus offered him a cup of blood. Then the prophet looked into the future and predicted what would happen next to Odysseus.

"Royal Odysseus, you seek a smooth journey home, but Poseidon, whose son you blinded, will make it hard for you," said Tiresias. "And beware the danger awaiting you on the island where the sacred cattle of the Sun live." These beasts were the most beautiful cattle in the world. According to Tiresias, if Odysseus' men harmed the cattle, they would be killed, and Odysseus would not return home for many years.

Tiresias continued on in his gloomy fashion. "When you do arrive home, you will find many troublemakers residing at your palace. But you will banish them and restore order."

After Tiresias finished speaking, many other ghosts came to drink blood and talk with Odysseus. He spoke with his mother, who had died of loneliness waiting for him to return. She told him that his wife, Penelope, still waited for him. Odysseus tried to embrace his mother. But because she was a ghost, his arms passed right through her. Heroes such as Patroclus and Achilles also approached Odysseus. But Ajax, still jealous that Odysseus had received Achilles' armor, refused to speak a single word to Odysseus.

More and more of the dead clustered around Odysseus, wanting to speak with him. Suddenly, he was hemmed in by thousands of ghosts, raising eerie, unearthly cries. As powerful as he was, Odysseus felt terror. He fled to his ship and urged his men to cast off at once. Mighty rowing and a fair wind sped them on their way, away from the kingdom of the dead and toward Ithaca.

QUESTIONS AND ANSWERS

Q: *Where did Odysseus go after he left the Cyclopes?*

A: He stopped at the Land of the Winds. King Aeolus gave him a leather bag that contained the strongest, most dangerous winds. He warned Odysseus not to open the bag, but some of his crew did anyway. The winds were released and drove the ship to the land of the Laestrygonians.

Q: *Where did Circe live?*

A: She lived in a palace on the island of Aeaea.

Q: *What were Circe's powers and how did Odysseus escape them?*

A: She was a witch who gave Odysseus' men a drugged potion and turned them into pigs. Hermes gave Odysseus an herb which protected him from Circe's powers. He drank her potion unharmed, which no man had ever done before.

Q: *Then what did Odysseus do?*

A: He forced Circe to turn his crew back into men, and they stayed there for a year.

Q: *What did Circe tell Odysseus he needed to do in order to return home?*

A: He had to go to the Underworld to meet with the prophet Tiresias.

Q: *What happened when Odysseus visited the Underworld?*

A: He sacrificed a ram and some sheep and filled a pit with their blood, because that was what the ghosts of the Underworld craved. Tiresias then appeared and told him not to eat any of the cattle on the Island of the Sun. Odysseus also visited with the ghosts of his mother and Achilles.

EXPERT COMMENTARY

The tradition of xenia, hospitality shown to guests, played an important part in how Odysseus and his men were driven to the land of Circe. According to Professor Barry B. Powell, "Aeolus feasts Odysseus and his men and gives him a special gift in accordance with the customs of xenia—a sealed cow-hide bag that contained the dangerous winds—which he warns him not to untie under any conditions."[5] The men, of course, untie the bag when Odysseus is asleep, release the winds, and drive the ships back to Aeolus. Powell noted that Aeolus offered them no further hospitality: "Observing that they must be bitterly hated by the gods to have suffered such a fate, Aeolus gruffly orders them away."[6]

Opening the bag of winds, according to Powell, was "another instance of the motif of the folktale prohibition."[7] Writers Kevin Osborn and Dana L. Burgess agreed:

> Many of the fantastic elements in the story of Odysseus' wan-derings seem more akin to the fairy tales of the Brothers Grimm than to the lofty legends of Greek gods and heroes. The foul-tempered Cyclops is not unlike the troll who blocks the Billy-Goats Gruff or the giant who chased Jack down the beanstalk. In the tale of Aeolus, we see that "curiosity killed the cat"—a common theme found in folk tales from Pandora to Goldilocks.[8]

Historian Michael Grant noted that the *Odyssey*, contrary to the *Iliad*, has many links to folktales:

> The *Odyssey* is a collection of folk-tales and fairy-tales: the fictitious stories, less sophisticated half-sisters of myth—"back-yard mythology," because they seem to have been handed down for entertainment rather than with the more solemn and purposeful motives or overtones which have given many other myths their power. The *Iliad* was a legend with a basis, how-ever tenuous, of fact; in the *Odyssey*, though, it describes the adventurous saga of a person believed historical (and linked to the Trojan War), we find the products not of memory, still less of reason, but of imagination—neither factual nor explanatory.[9]

8

DEADLY DANGERS ON THE SEA

INTRODUCTION

In this tale, Odysseus and his crew sailed back to Aeaea where Circe, the sorceress, used her magical powers to find out about three deadly dangers that lay ahead: the Sirens, Scylla, and Charybdis. First, Odysseus had to steer his ship safely by the Sirens, who lured unsuspecting sailors to their deaths. Then, he would encounter Scylla, a six-headed monster, and Charybdis, a deadly whirlpool. If he and his crew made it safely through these dangers, they would land on the Island of the Sun. Circe told Odysseus that no matter how hungry he and his men were, none of them should touch the cattle of the Sun. Anyone who touched them would never return home.

The tales of the Sirens, Scylla, and Charybdis are based on stories well-known to Homer's listeners. The hero Jason and his crew, the Argonauts, faced these same dangers in a Greek myth that is older than the *Iliad* and the *Odyssey*.[1] In the twelfth book of the *Odyssey*, knowledge of Jason's voyage and his adventures is assumed.

A key theme of this tale is that of a fantastic journey. It retells many fantastic and amazing adventures that Odysseus faced. The stories of Circe and the Cyclops are other stories with this theme.

The nymph, Calypso, who appears in this myth, represents other divine and mortal women who fell in love with Odysseus. Most of them, including Calypso, tried to entrap him, often by trickery. Faced with the temptations these women presented, such as beauty and luxurious living, the mighty hero ultimately resisted the love of all the women other than his wife.

The love of Odysseus for his wife and son plays an important part in this tale. Although at first he enjoyed the relaxing life on Calypso's island, especially after ten years of war, Odysseus longed deeply for Penelope and Telemachus. This longing led to his ultimate release from Calypso's island.

DEADLY DANGERS
ON THE SEA

The Sirens sang high, thrilling songs that bewitched sailors and caused them to crash their ships into the rocks. They were surrounded by the whitened bones of their many victims. To prevent his crew from hearing the Sirens' voices, Odysseus cut a circular chunk of beeswax into pieces, softened the pieces, and plugged the ears of his crew members with the wax. But Odysseus wanted to hear the songs of the Sirens, so he commanded his men, "Bind me hand and foot and tie me to the mast, for I want to hear the music of these maidens. But I dare not take a chance of having our last remaining ship crash into the cliffs, so I must be lashed to the mast. No matter how hard I urge you, do not release me until we are safely out of reach of the Sirens."

As the ship drew near to the Sirens, they burst into song. "Come closer to us, famous Odysseus," they sang. "Moor your ship near our coast so that you can listen to our sweet songs forever."

Odysseus strained against the ropes that bound him to the mast. He signaled frantically to his crew to set him free, but they followed Odysseus' command and refused to release him. They flung themselves against the oars and rowed harder and harder until the voices of the Sirens faded away. When the crew felt that they were out of danger, they removed the wax in their ears and loosed Odysseus' bonds.

No sooner had they escaped from the Sirens when

Odysseus spied waves booming against another set of cliffs. The passageway between them was so narrow that it seemed impossible to pass through. In a cave on the higher cliff lived Scylla, a long-necked monster with six dogs' heads and twelve feet. When ships passed by, she stretched out her feet and grabbed sailors from their decks. She tore them to pieces with her many sharp teeth so that they died a terrible death.

Below the cliff directly opposite Scylla lived Charybdis, a deadly whirlpool, that sucked in the water of the passageway three times a day. Then, she spit it out in towering spouts. When a ship entered the whirling spiral, none on board survived. Sometimes, a lucky ship would pass over the whirlpool when she was calm, but the chances of this happening were rare. Odysseus decided that sailing near Charybdis meant certain death for everyone on the ship, so he sailed closer to Scylla. Still, even though his crew rowed furiously, Scylla snatched and ate six of the men.

By this time, Odysseus' sailors had been rowing for weeks without food and were starving. They landed on the Island of the Sun to rest. Odysseus made them swear they would leave the cattle untouched. At first, they caught fish and hunted game. But their increasing hunger drove the men to a foolish action. When Odysseus went to sleep, the men could not resist killing and roasting several of the cattle. When Odysseus awoke, he was horrified, for he knew his men would be punished. After the ship set sail again, Zeus took revenge. He sent a thunderbolt which destroyed the ship and sent it spinning to the bottom of the ocean, carrying everyone but Odysseus to their deaths.

For nine days, Odysseus drifted on the sea by clinging to the mast and keel, or bottom, of his ship. On the tenth day, he washed ashore on Ogyia, the island home of the beautiful nymph, Calypso. The long-haired nymph nursed him back to health and fell in love with Odysseus in the process. She planned to keep him with her forever. Without a ship, Odysseus could not escape her island. Calypso plied

Odysseus with fine food and drink to tempt him to stay with her. She offered him immortality and eternal youth. She made life so comfortable for him that he stayed on her island for seven years and did not do a single day's work the entire time. Yet although Calypso begged him to stay with her, Odysseus could not forget Penelope. He began to feel sharp pangs of loneliness for his home and family.

Poseidon, who did not want Odysseus to reach home, rejoiced in the hero's homesickness. However, Athena decided it was time for Odysseus to receive his wish: to see his wife and son again. Athena waited until Poseidon was occupied somewhere else. Then, she visited Zeus and asked him to command Calypso to let Odysseus go.

Zeus sent his messenger, Hermes, to tell Calypso to release Odysseus. Hermes strapped on his golden, winged sandals and flew over the waves to Calypso's island. He entered the cave where the nymph with the lovely braids made her home. With a breathtaking voice, she sang as she wove colorful cloths at her loom deep inside the cave.

Calypso recognized Hermes right away. "Messenger god, my dear friend, why have you come?" she asked. "I am eager to do whatever you wish." She asked Hermes to sit at a table, where she served him ambrosia and roasted meats.

When Hermes had finished eating, he said, "Zeus bade me come. The king of the gods claims that you are keeping beside you Odysseus, a man who set sail for home after helping win the Trojan War. On the way, he faced many adventures and lost all of his men. Now Zeus commands you to let him go, for it is not his fate to die here."

At first, Calypso was angry at these words. "I saved Odysseus from drowning after Zeus had destroyed his ship with one white-hot lightning bolt. Now the king of the gods wishes me to let Odysseus go?" Calypso sighed in frustration. "I will send Odysseus off, since this is the will of Zeus."

Hermes flew back to Olympus and Calypso searched for Odysseus to tell him the news that he was going home. She

found him sitting on the beach, weeping because he was so homesick.

"Kind Calypso," he said, "I am forever grateful that you saved me from certain death in the sea. But I am so lonely for my wife and son."

"There is no need for you to grieve for them any longer, Odysseus," Calypso said. "Zeus has commanded that you are to return to Ithaca. I am willing, heart and soul, to send you home now."

She invited him back to her cave for a farewell feast before he left. Despite her fervent promise to let Odysseus go, Calypso wanted one more chance to try to convince him to stay with her.

"So, Odysseus," Calypso said as she sipped her cup of ambrosia. "Are you still eager to hurry back to Ithaca? If you only knew what pain your departure causes me. If you stay with me, I will make you immortal. Even though your lovely wife, Penelope, is faithful and true, she will not live forever."

"Beautiful nymph," Odysseus answered, "what you say is true. Yet, if I do not leave now, I will long for the rest of my days for a glimpse of the shores of Ithaca and the family that waits for me there."

So Calypso gave Odysseus a bronze ax and adze, a tool for shaping wood. She led him to the edge of her island where the trees grew tall, perfect for constructing a raft. Odysseus cut twenty sturdy timbers and split them into planks. He bored holes through the planks with drills and joined them together with pegs. Then, he added a mast and an oar to help steer him along the best course home. After four days of work, the raft was ready.

On the morning of the fifth day, Calypso joined Odysseus at the shore to launch the raft. She gave him water and wine and her choicest meats to take along. Then, she summoned a gentle breeze to send him on his way. With the wind lifting his spirits, Odysseus pointed his raft toward home.

QUESTIONS AND ANSWERS

Q: *How did Odysseus handle the dangerous Sirens?*

A: He plugged the ears of his men so that they could not hear the Sirens' songs. Odysseus was lashed to the mast of his ship so that he could hear the music, but could not yield to it.

Q: *Describe the dangers of Scylla and Charybdis. Did Odysseus avoid these dangers?*

A: Scylla was a monster with six dogs' heads and twelve feet. She grabbed sailors from their ships as they passed by. Charybdis sucked water from the passageway and spit it out in towering spouts. Odysseus sailed near Scylla and she ate six of his men.

Q: *What happened on the Island of the Sun?*

A: Odysseus' men were so hungry that they killed some of the sacred cattle on the island. When the ship set sail after this, Zeus sent a thunderbolt that destroyed the ship and killed all the men except Odysseus.

Q: *How did Odysseus survive?*

A: For several days, he clung to the mast and keel of the ship. Then, he was cast ashore onto the island of Calypso.

Q: *How long did Odysseus stay on the island? Why?*

A: He was there for seven years, because he did not have a ship to escape.

Q: *Was Odysseus happy with Calypso?*

A: He enjoyed the leisure life on the island, but he missed his wife and son.

Q: *How did Odysseus finally leave the island?*

A: Zeus ordered Calypso to let Odysseus go. She helped him build a raft, and he sailed away.

EXPERT COMMENTARY

Scylla was not always a deadly monster:

> Scylla was once a beautiful but aloof maiden, the beloved of
> Glaucus, a sea god. Glaucus asked Circe to prepare a potion
> that would cause Scylla to fall in love with him. Circe, herself
> enamored with Glaucus, attempted to seduce him, but the sea
> god could think only of Scylla. So instead of a love potion, the
> jealous sorceress gave Glaucus a potion that transformed his
> beloved into a grotesque monster.[2]

The story of the Sirens appears in the writings of several
ancient authors. However, according to classicists Mark P. O.
Morford and Robert J. Lenardon, the Sirens were "said by
Homer to be two in number, but by other authors to be
more."[3]

In his voyage home, Odysseus had to resist not only the
temptations of the Sirens, but also many other dangers:

> The way in which Odysseus resists the deadly pleasure of the
> Sirens recalls his own forbearance among the Lotus-Eaters.
> Odysseus not only faces the challenge of conquering giants
> and ogres in his quest to return to Penelope. The hero must
> also deny himself the delights of the lotus, Circe, the Sirens,
> and later Calypso—or he will never make it home.[4]

One of the themes of the *Odyssey* is that of the hero who
wants to find his way home. According to classicist Bernard
Knox:

> Many centuries after Homer, the Florentine Dante Alighieri,
> who had not read Homer and whose information about
> Ulysses (the Latin form of Odysseus' name) came from Virgil
> and Ovid, saw in the Greek hero a vision of the restless explor-
> er, the man who, discontented with the mundane life of that
> home he had longed for, set off again in search of new worlds.[5]

Knox observed that Homer's view of Odysseus is quite
different: "But these visions of Odysseus as the restless
explorer, hungry for new worlds, have little to do with

Homer's Odysseus, who wants above all things to find his way home and stay there."[6] Beginning in the ancient world, many geographers tried to plot Odysseus' journey:

> This wild-goose chase had begun already in the ancient world, as we know from the brusque dismissal of such identifications by the great Alexandrian geographer Eratosthenes, who said that you would be able to chart the course of Odysseus' wanderings when you found the cobbler who sewed the bag in which Aeolus confined the winds. This of course has not deterred modern scholars and amateurs from trying; their guesses run from the possible—Charybdis as a mythical personification of whirlpools in the straits between Sicily and the toe of the Italian boot—to the fantastic: Calypso's island as Iceland."[7]

During his voyage, Odysseus often depended on the kindness of strangers, according to classicist Bernard Knox:

> Some of them, like the Phaeacians and Aeolus, king of the winds, will be perfect hosts, entertaining him lavishly and sending him on his way with precious gifts. Others will be savages, threatening his life and taking the lives of his crew. Still others will be importunate hosts, delaying the guest's departure—an infraction of the code. . . . Circe is a charming hostess, but she charms her guests out of human shape and keeps them forever. Calypso too would have kept Odysseus forever, but in his own shape, perpetually young. The Sirens would have kept him forever also, but dead. Calypso and Circe, however, when the time comes to speed the parting guest, provide the requisite gifts. Calypso sends a fair wind to send his raft on its way, and Circe gives him precious instructions—how to deal with the Sirens, the warning not to kill the cattle of the Sun.[8]

9

HOME AT LAST

INTRODUCTION

One of the themes of this story is that a soldier who returns home from war must also reconquer his homeland. As a returning warrior, Odysseus must re-establish his position in the household. This meant driving out the more than 100 suitors who pestered his wife, stole his property, and threatened his son.

Another theme is that of a young boy maturing into a young man. When Odysseus left home to fight in the Trojan War, his son, Telemachus, was an infant. Throughout the *Odyssey*, Telemachus developed independence and self-confidence as he helped his parents. Athena assisted him in his education by sending him to Sparta and other foreign lands. When his father returned home, Telemachus learned how to implement a battle plan and stood at his father's side, killing all the suitors.

Penelope represented the ideal of Greek womanhood. She waited faithfully for her husband, no matter what he did. She operated a complex household with skill, despite the threat that came from the presence of the suitors. Penelope also demonstrated intelligence, for in this tale, she tested Odysseus before she would acknowledge him as her husband returned home from the war.

The Greek concept of xenia also played an important part in this myth, as it has in the stories of the judgment of Paris, the Cyclops, and Circe. A stranger was always welcomed by the host. Serving girls anointed, or rubbed, the guest's body with olive oil and provided him with fresh clothing. Then, the guest would tell of his family and his journey. Above all, a guest was never to harm his host. A host, in turn, was always to act honorably to his guest. The Phaeacians offered hospitality to Odysseus. Then, the Phaeacians set sail to return home to Scheria. Unfortunately, Poseidon was so furious with them for helping Odysseus that he turned the ship and crew into stone as they approached their own harbor. As a result, the Phaeacians never again offered hospitality to strangers.

HOME AT LAST

More danger awaited Odysseus. Poseidon saw him as his raft neared the land of the Phaeacians, a kind people known for being skilled sailors. The god of the sea was furious that Zeus had helped his enemy, Odysseus. Poseidon sent down a huge storm that destroyed the tiny raft. However, the sea goddess Leucothea gave Odysseus her veil. She told him to wrap it around his waist to help keep him afloat and to swim with all his might. After two days and nights, Odysseus reached the shores of Scheria, home of the Phaeacians. He tossed the veil back into the sea and, exhausted, crawled under some bushes to sleep.

The next day, the Princess Nausicaä found him when she went to wash clothes down by the shore. She brought him to her father, King Alcinoüs. The king was known for his hospitality to strangers. Alcinoüs gave Odysseus many precious guest gifts, such as cauldrons filled with silver and garments trimmed with gold. He also gave him a ship and some of his best sailors to take him back to Ithaca.

Once on board ship, Odysseus fell so soundly asleep that the sailors did not want to disturb him. When they arrived at Ithaca, the Phaeacians left Odysseus asleep on the shore, surrounded by the gifts that King Alcinoüs had sent him.

When Odysseus awakened, he did not recognize where he was because he had been away from Ithaca for twenty years. Athena, disguised as a herdsman, appeared to him and reassured him that he was finally home safely. She helped him hide the treasures in a cave. Then, she transformed the mighty warrior into an old beggar in tattered rags. She touched him with her wand and changed his skin into that of an old man. Then she said, "I will be with you when you confront the greedy suitors at your palace. But do not go immediately to the palace. First, visit Eumaeus, your faithful swineherd." This herder of pigs lived in a hut out in the country. "Stay with him until you find out exactly what has happened at the palace while you have been gone. I will go and fetch your son, Telemachus, from Sparta."

Eumaeus did not recognize Odysseus, for his disguise was excellent. But the rules of xenia dictated that he must offer hospitality to a stranger. He offered his best food and drink to the beggar. Then Odysseus, still disguised as a beggar, asked Eumaeus what the situation was like at the palace.

"The suitors, more than one hundred in number, devour the wealth of Odysseus. They eat his animals and waste his wine with their riotous living," complained Eumaeus. "Yet, Penelope remains true to her husband and waits anxiously for his return. But come, it is time for sleep. Please, as my guest, take the place of honor near the fire. I will sleep outside. That way, I can be sure that no harm will come to you."

Odysseus was honored that his servant had been so faithful and treated him as a honored guest. But Odysseus was not yet ready to reveal himself to Eumaeus.

In the meantime, a perilous situation had developed for Odysseus' family on Ithaca. It had been twenty years since Odysseus had sailed for Troy. His baby son was now grown up. By now, everyone except his family and his trusted servants thought that Odysseus was dead. The general feeling was that Penelope should remarry, since she was queen of a rich land. Many suitors desired the wealth and power that would come with being ruler of Ithaca. They had come from all the nearby islands to try to convince Penelope to marry one of them. They spent many hours sitting in the great hall of the palace, eating and drinking the food and wine that by rights belonged to Odysseus. Even worse, the suitors were rude to Penelope and threatened to harm Telemachus.

At first, Penelope tricked the suitors. She concocted a scheme which she hoped would drive her suitors to boredom and cause them to leave. "I cannot marry again until I have woven a very fine burial garment to cover the body of Laertes, the father of Odysseus. I must have this ready before Laertes dies," she said.

As rude as the suitors had been, none of them were rude enough to criticize such a task. Little did they know that each night, Penelope picked apart what she had woven during the day. Penelope carried on this scheme for three years until a disloyal servant told the suitors what she was doing. As a result, the suitors pestered Penelope even more to choose one of them to marry. This was the situation when Odysseus landed on Ithaca at the end of his ten years of wandering.

Just before Odysseus had arrived on Ithaca, Athena had sent Telemachus to Pylos and Sparta. There, he learned about leadership from the kings and warriors Nestor and Menelaus. Then, Athena told him he needed to return to Ithaca, for his father was there. She also cautioned him that the suitors planned to ambush him upon his return, so he landed on the opposite side of the island from where they expected him. Then, Telemachus went to Eumaeus' hut, where the swineherd welcomed him with tears of rejoicing.

Odysseus, still in his beggar's rags, approached Telemachus. Then, Athena turned Odysseus back into his royal self. He stood before his son in purple robes and shining armor. The two hugged each other and wept tears of joy.

But their celebrating was short, for they had to plan what to do about the suitors. They decided to return to the palace with Odysseus dressed again as a beggar. Their strategy was to wait for the suitors to fall asleep drunk as they did each night. Then, Odysseus and Telemachus would hide the suitors' weapons, so that they would be defenseless.

Still not revealing his identity, Odysseus entered the

palace and begged among the suitors. Some gave him food. However, one of them threw a footstool at Odysseus and threatened him.

Penelope, however, would not allow anyone to be insulted or mistreated in her home. She asked the beggar how he had come to Ithaca and what his reasons were for visiting. He said, "Many years ago, I met your husband in Troy. He spoke so well of you that I knew I would be received in kindness." He described precisely an unusual brooch, or pin, that Odysseus wore at his neck.

Penelope cried when she heard the description of the brooch, because it reminded her how much she missed Odysseus. As much as he wanted to, though, Odysseus did not comfort her and identify himself, for the time was not yet right to do this. However, he told her that he had heard that Odysseus was in a nearby land, alive and well.

Before retiring for the night, Penelope asked Euryclea, who had been Odysseus' childhood nurse, to wash the feet of the beggar. Euryclea filled a bronze cauldron with hot water. As she scrubbed the beggar's feet and legs, she felt a scar on his thigh and recognized it as a hunting injury Odysseus had received as a child. Odysseus warned her not to reveal his identity.

The next day, Athena set in motion the circumstances in which Odysseus would banish the suitors. She gave Penelope the idea that she should set up a contest to choose one of the suitors to marry. Odysseus owned a bow and set of arrows that was so powerful that no one else could use it. It had been stored in a closet while Odysseus was gone. Penelope would marry the suitor who could string the bow and shoot an arrow through a row of twelve axes.

In preparation for the contest, a feast was set up in the dining hall. Telemachus, Eumaeus, and Philoetius, another faithful servant, pretended to help with the preparations. But in reality, they were ready to help Odysseus kill the suitors. Telemachus did not want his mother to witness the bloody slaughter, so he sent her to bed.

The contest began. Not one of the suitors was even able to string the bow. Then, from the corner of the room came the voice of the beggar. "Every man here has had an opportunity to try his hand at this contest, I would like to try my hand at it, as well."

Of course, all the suitors mocked him. How could an old beggar succeed where none of them had?

Telemachus, on the other hand, knew that once his father held the bow, he could shoot each of the suitors. He stood behind his father and handed him an arrow. Odysseus, of course, shot it through all the axes with absolutely no difficulty. Then, Odysseus stripped himself of all his rags and emptied the quiver, or case, of arrows at his feet. Ready for shooting, he addressed the astounded suitors. "So ends this meaningless contest, for now I shall shoot at another target and hit it, if Apollo grants my prayer."

Odysseus aimed a deadly arrow at the rudest suitor, killing him with one shot. Telemachus, Eumaeus, and Philoetius joined in the fighting. In no time, they had killed all the greedy, disagreeable suitors.

Finally, Odysseus was able to reveal who he was to Penelope. But she wanted to be sure of his identity. To test Odysseus, she told the servants to remove their bed from the room and put it in the hall.

Odysseus looked at her in surprise. "Penelope, the bed cannot be moved. Not even a god could shift it. I know for I built it myself and built the bedroom around it. Its headboard is an olive tree whose roots are anchored deep in the ground."

Penelope cried out in joy, for the only people who knew the secret of the bed were Odysseus, Euryclea, and Penelope herself. She rushed to Odysseus, flung her arms around his neck, and kissed him over and over again. Soon the entire palace was filled with rejoicing over the homecoming of the mighty warrior.

QUESTIONS AND ANSWERS

Q: *What happened when Poseidon discovered Odysseus sailing on his raft?*

A: He sent a huge storm to destroy it. But Odysseus washed ashore on the island of the Phaeacians.

Q: *How did Athena help Odysseus when he awoke?*

A: She told him that he was safely home in Ithaca. She helped him store his treasure in a cave. Then, she disguised him as a beggar.

Q: *Where did Odysseus go next?*

A: He went to the hut of Eumaeus, his faithful swineherd. Although Eumaeus did not recognize Odysseus in his disguise, he offered him hospitality.

Q: *What was the situation at the palace at that time?*

A: Suitors had come from all over the islands to try to convince Penelope to marry one of them. The suitors wanted the wealth and power that would come from being king of Ithaca. They sat around the palace, eating and drinking, and acting rudely.

Q: *What scheme did Penelope use to try to drive away the suitors? Did this trick work?*

A: She told them she could not marry until she finished weaving a funeral robe for Odysseus' father. Every night, she picked out what she had woven the previous day. However, an unfaithful servant told the suitors what Penelope was doing. The suitors then pestered Penelope to make a decision to marry one of them.

Q: *Why did Telemachus go to Pylos and Sparta?*

A: Athena wanted him to learn about leadership qualities, which he would need to help his father.

Q: *What was the contest Penelope devised to choose one of the suitors?*

A: She would marry the one who could string Odysseus' mighty bow and shoot an arrow through twelve axes in a row.

Q: *What happened when the suitors tried to string the bow?*

A: None of them was strong enough.

Q: *Odysseus, disguised as a beggar, then asked for a chance to try. What happened?*

A: The suitors made fun of him. However, he was successful on his first try. Then, he shot another arrow at the rudest suitor, killing him immediately.

Q: *Who joined Odysseus in fighting the suitors and what was the result?*

A: Telemachus, Eumaeus, and Philoetius joined Odysseus in killing all the suitors.

EXPERT COMMENTARY

Professor Seth L. Schein compared the two Homeric epics:

> Unlike the *Iliad*, the *Odyssey* is not confined to a setting of war and death: its hero journeys far and wide through the real world and lands of fantasy, unreality, and half-reality in his effort to reach home and family. En route, he several times explicitly contrasts himself to those heroes who died at Troy, and on other occasions the poem calls attention both to how he differs from Achilles and the other Iliadic heroes and to how the Trojan War is but a part of the experiences that make him who and what he is.[1]

According to Professor Schein, the entire concept of what it means to be a hero differs in the two Homeric epics:

> . . . the *Odyssey* is about what it means to be human. On the other hand, the particular ways in which Odysseus is represented as heroic and human and Ithaca is represented as his home and the source, goal, and scene of his heroism, differ from the ways in which heroism and the human condition are represented in the *Iliad*. In recent years scholars have come to think of these differences as characteristic not only of the poems themselves but of distinct Iliadic and Odyssean traditions within the overall poetic tradition.[2]

Professor Barry B. Powell noted that:

> In ancient times the *Iliad* was compared to tragedy because of its somber themes and deep personal conflict; the *Odyssey*, by contrast, was compared with comedy because . . . it has a happy ending in which the family is reunited and the promise of the future is affirmed. The *Odyssey* is a towering artistic achievement, admired and still imitated by artists today.[3]

Penelope played an important role in the *Odyssey*. After noting that Odysseus remained faithful to Penelope, scholars Mark P. O. Morford and Robert J. Lenardon observed:

> The reunion with his wife is the goal of the epic. Penelope is not a passive figure: she is the equal of Odysseus in

intelligence and loyalty, and she is resourceful in fending off the suitors and, equally significant, in choosing her time and method for the recognition of Odysseus. When she finally does recognize him the poet describes her "as fitting his heart" (*thymares*), that is, she is a perfect match for the man who is the "man of many twists and turns" (*polytropos*, an epithet given him in the first line of the poem), the cleverest of the Greeks.[4]

Classicist Michael Grant also noted that the *Odyssey* has deep ties with folklore:

The *Odyssey* is cast in the form of an epic. But its basis is a widespread folk-tale: that of the man so long absent that he is given up for dead, yet finally, after he has successfully sought and found his home again, reunited with his faithful wife.[5]

Grant commented on the theme of the *Odyssey*:

Finding what is lost, the *Odyssey's* basic subject, is a powerful theme of the world's great writers, and one which is very prominent in Greek and Roman mythology. It is the core of Shakespeare's later plays, *Cymbeline*, *The Winter's Tale*, *The Tempest*, and *Pericles*. Royalty is what is lost there, and it serves as a symbol of the deeper spiritual search. The power-quest also dominates the mythologies, for example, of North American Indians. . . . At any rate the Quest was imprinted very early in our human minds and hearts—and the *Odyssey* is its supreme manifestation.[6]

🔲 GLOSSARY 🔲

adze—A tool for shaping wood.

ambrosia—The food of the gods.

arete—The ancient Greek concept of striving for excellence, a particular goal of heroes.

cauldron—A large pot.

cosmopolitan—Having a broader, more world-wide mixture.

epic—A long poem that tells the deeds of a hero or heroes in elegant, formal language.

fate—The belief that life's outcomes are predetermined by the gods.

hubris—Excessive pride. Heroes in Greek mythology who demonstrated excessive pride often made tragic decisions.

Ilium—Another name for Troy.

keel—The bottom of a ship.

kleos—The Greek word referring to the glory sought by a hero.

lays—Short narrative poems combined to form longer epics. Some historians believe that the Greek epics were composed of lays.

moly—The herb that Hermes gave Odysseus to protect him from Circe's magic.

mythos—The Greek word for story, tale, or speech.

Nostoi—The Greek word for returns or homecoming. The journeys of the Greek leaders other than Odysseus were recorded in an epic of this title, which is now lost.

nymph—A minor goddess or divinity of nature. Nymphs usually dwelled in the mountains, forests, trees, or water. They were often portrayed as young women.

Odusseia—Greek word meaning the story of Odysseus.

odyssey—A journey or quest; usually a long, wandering voyage filled with many changes of fortune.

oracle—A prophet or prophetess who foretold the future.

papyrus—An Egyptian plant cut into strips and pressed to make a paper-type material.

pestilence—Disease.

polis—The Greek city-state, an independent self-governing community.

pyre—A bed of materials that are collected into a tall pile onto which a body is placed and burned at a funeral.

quiver—A case for carrying arrows.

sack—To loot and destroy a city.

theomachies—Two episodes in the *Iliad* in which the gods fight each other on the battlefield.

urn—A vase used to hold the ashes of a person who has died.

vellum—A fine-grained animal skin used for making books.

▣ CHAPTER NOTES ▣

Preface

1. D.S. Carne-Ross, "The Poem of Odysseus," in Robert Fitzgerald, translator, *Homer: The Odyssey* (New York: Farrar, Straus and Giroux, Inc., 1998), p. ix.

2. Michael Grant, *Myths of the Greeks and Romans* (New York: Meridian, 1995), p. 29.

3. Ibid., p. 54.

4. Bernard Knox, "Introduction," in Robert Fagles, translator, *Homer: The Iliad* (New York: Penguin Books, 1999), p. 7.

5. Seth L. Schein, "Introduction," in Seth L. Schein, ed., *Reading the Odyssey* (Princeton, N.J.: Princeton University Press, 1996), p. 3.

6. Bernard Knox, "Introduction," in Robert Fagles, translator, *Homer: The Odyssey*, (New York: Penguin Books, 1996), p. 18.

7. Ibid.

8. Knox, *Iliad*, p. 19.

9. Ibid., p. 21; Knox, *Odyssey*, p. 20.

10. Knox, *Iliad*, p. 6.

11. Schein, p. 3.

Chapter 1. The Judgment of Paris

1. Lucilla Burn, *Greek Myths* (Austin, Tex.: University of Texas Press, 1990), p. 31.

2. Bernard Knox, "Introduction," in Robert Fagles, translator, *Homer: The Iliad* (New York: Penguin Books, 1999), p. 41.

3. Ibid., p. 24.

4. Ibid., p. 30.

5. Ibid., p. 31.

6. Barry B. Powell, *Classical Myth*, 2nd. ed. (Upper Saddle River, N.J.: Prentice Hall, 1998), pp. 510-511.

7. Knox, p. 42.

Chapter 2. Achilles Argues with Agamemnon

1. Michael Grant, *Myths of the Greeks and Romans* (New York: Meridian, 1995), p. 32.

2. Robert Fagles, translator, *Homer: The Iliad* (New York: Penguin Books, 1990), p. 77.

3. Grant, p. 33.

4. Fagles, p. 449.

5. Bernard Knox, "Introduction," in Robert Fagles' *Homer: The Iliad* (New York: Penguin Books, 1990), p. 24.

6. Ibid., p. 25.

7. Roberto Calasso, *The Marriage of Cadmus and Harmony*, trans. Tim Parks (Toronto, Canada: Vintage Books Canada, 1994), p. 105.

8. Barry B. Powell, *Classical Myth*, 2nd. ed. (Upper Saddle River, N.J.: Prentice Hall, 1998), p. 511.

9. Ibid., p. 512.

10. Mark P. O. Morford and Robert J. Lenardon, *Classical Mythology*, 6th ed. (New York: Addison-Wesley Educational Publishers Inc., 1999), p. 364.

Chapter 3. Achilles Versus Hector

1. Michael Grant, *Myths of the Greeks and Romans* (New York: Meridian, 1995), p. 37.

2. Mark P. O. Morford and Robert J. Lenardon, *Classical Mythology*, 6th ed. (New York: Addison-Wesley Educational Publishers Inc., 1999), pp. 378-379.

3. Ibid., p. 377.

4. Robert Fagles, translator, *Homer: The Iliad* (New York: Penguin Books, 1990), p. 633.

5. Ibid., p. 622.

Chapter 4. The Trojan Horse

1. Robert Graves, *The Greek Myths*, complete ed. (New York: Penguin Books, 1992), p. 697.

2. Barry B. Powell, *Classical Myth*, 2nd. ed. (Upper Saddle River, N.J.: Prentice Hall, 1998), p. 538.

3. Ibid., 540.

Chapter 5. The Lotus-Eaters

1. *Webster's Ninth New Collegiate Dictionary* (Springfield, Mass.: Merriam-Webster, Inc., Publishers, 1984), p. 818.

2. Bernard Knox, "Introduction," in Robert Fagles, trans., *Homer: The Odyssey* (New York: Penguin Books, 1996), p. 3.

3. Barry B. Powell, *Classical Myth*, 2nd. ed. (Upper Saddle River, N.J.: Prentice Hall, 1998), p. 559.

4. Ibid.

5. Ibid.

6. Ibid., p. 532.

Chapter 6. The Cyclops

1. Iain Thomson, *Ancient Greek Mythology* (Edison, N.J.: Chartwell Books, Inc., 1996), p. 55.

2. Barry B. Powell, *Classical Myth*, 2nd. ed. (Upper Saddle River, N.J.: Prentice Hall, 1998), p. 580.

3. Ibid., p. 564.

4. Ibid.

5. Ibid.

6. Michael Grant, *Myths of the Greeks and Romans* (New York: Meridian, 1995), p. 72.

7. Ibid., pp. 68-69.

8. Ibid., p. 69.

Chapter 7. Circe, the Bewitching Queen

1. Robert Fagles, translator, *Homer: The Odyssey* (New York: Penguin, 1996), p. 230.

2. Barry B. Powell, *Classical Myth*, 2nd. ed. (Upper Saddle River, N.J.: Prentice Hall, 1998), p. 572.

3. Ibid.

4. Mark P. O. Morford and Robert J. Lenardon, *Classical Mythology*, 6th ed. (New York: Addison-Wesley Educational Publishers Inc., 1999), p. 393.

5. Powell, p. 569.

6. Ibid.

7. Ibid.

8. Kevin Osborn and Dana L. Burgess, *The Complete Idiot's Guide to Classical Mythology* (New York: Prentice-Hall, Inc., 1998), p. 222.

9. Michael Grant, *Myths of the Greeks and Romans* (New York: Meridian, 1995), p. 72.

Chapter 8. Deadly Dangers on the Sea

1. Karen B. Spies, *Heroes in Greek Mythology* (Berkeley Heights, N.J.: Enslow Publishers, 2002), p. 55.

2. Kevin Osborn and Dana L. Burgess, *The Complete Idiot's Guide to Classical Mythology* (New York: Prentice-Hall, Inc., 1998), p. 255.

3. Mark P. O. Morford and Robert J. Lenardon, *Classical Mythology*, 6th ed. (New York: Addison-Wesley Educational Publishers Inc., 1999), p. 395.

4. Osborn and Burgess, p. 225.

5. Bernard Knox, "Introduction," in Robert Fagles, trans., *Homer: The Odyssey* (New York: Penguin Books, 1996), p. 25.

6. Ibid.

7. Ibid.

8. Ibid., pp. 30–31.

Chapter 9. Home at Last

1. Seth L. Schein, ed., *Reading The Odyssey* (Princeton, N.J.: Princeton University Press, 1996), p. 10.

2. Ibid., pp. 5–6.

3. Barry B. Powell, *Classical Myth*, 2nd. ed. (Upper Saddle River, N.J.: Prentice Hall, 1998), p. 556.

4. Mark P. O. Morford and Robert J. Lenardon, *Classical Mythology*, 6th ed. (New York: Addison-Wesley Educational Publishers Inc., 1999), p. 401.

5. Michael Grant, *Myths of the Greeks and Romans* (New York: Meridian, 1995), p. 72.

6. Ibid.

🔲 FURTHER READING 🔲

Colum, Padriac. *The Trojan War and the Adventures of Odysseus.* New York: William Morrow & Co., 1997.

Fagles, Robert, translator. *Homer: The Iliad.* New York: Penguin Books, 1990.

Fleischman, Paul. *Dateline: Troy.* Cambridge, Mass.: Candlewick Press, 1996.

Mattern, Joanne. *The Odyssey.* New York: HarperCollins Publishers, 1996.

Sutcliff, Rosemary. *Black Ships Before Troy: The Story of the Iliad.* New York: Delacorte Press, 1993.

Williams, Marcia, illustrator. *The Iliad and the Odyssey.* Cambridge, Mass.: Candlewick Press, 1998.

INTERNET ADDRESSES

The History of Greece and Greek Mythology

<http://www.ancientgreece.com>

The Perseus Encyclopedia: Homer

<http://www.perseus.tufts.edu/cgi-bin/text?lookup=
encyclopedia+Homer>

The Trojan War

<http://www.oup-usa.org/sc/0195143388/chaptertopics/
summary_17.html>

🔲 INDEX 🔲

A

Achaeans, 29–30
  and Patroclus, 39, 46, 48, 50
  and the Trojan horse, 58, 61
Achilles
  argument with Agamemnon,
    13, 28–43
  characteristics, 42–43, 53
  death, 45, 56, 63
  ghost, 55, 92, 93
  role in the *Iliad*, 31
  vs. Hector, 46–53, 62
Achilles heel, 31, 56
Aeneid, 55
Aeolus, 87, 88, 94, 105
Agamemnon of Mycenae, King
  argument with Achilles, 13, 31,
    33–43, 48
  command, 30
  rescue of Helen, 7
Ajax, 37–38, 55, 56, 57, 63, 92
Alcinoüs, King, 68, 108
Amazons, 30
Andromache, 55, 62
Aphrodite, 19–22, 25, 27, 36–37,
  45
Apollo, 33–34, 40, 56, 60–61, 63
Archaic Period, 11
Ares, 45
arete (excellence), 31, 118
Artemis, 27, 31, 45
Athena
  fighting Aphrodite and Ares, 45
  against Hector, 49
  helping Telemachus, 107
  and judgment of Paris, 19–22,
    27
  making Ajax insane, 57
  on Odysseus' return home,
    100, 108–109, 110, 111, 114
  punishment of the Greeks, 69,
    73
  and the Trojan horse, 60
Athens, 11, 12

B

Briseïs, 29, 36, 37, 38, 41

C

Calchas, 31, 34
Calypso, 96, 99–102, 103, 104, 105
Cassandra, 55, 60, 64, 69, 73
Charybdis, 96, 98, 103, 105
Chryseïs, 33–34
Chryses, 33–34
Circe, 86–94, 96, 105
Classical Period, 12
Cyclops, 77–85

D

Dark Age, 10–11
Deiphobus, 49, 62
Diomedes, 45, 57–58
Dorians, 10

E

epic, 5, 118
Ethiopians, 30
Eumaeus, 109, 111, 113, 114, 115
Euripides, 18, 55
Euryclea, 111, 113
Eurylochus, 89

F

Fates, 13

G

Greece, ancient
  archeology, 7–8
  language, 9
  map, 4
  peoples and history, 8–12
  political system, 11, 29
  religion and culture, 13, 26
  trade, 8, 9
Greek mythology, 45
  of the Classical Period, 12
  epics, 5
  in Greek art, 65

link to folktales, 94, 117
origins, 8

H

Hector, 30, 37, 40, 41, 46–53, 62
Helen
kidnapping by Paris, 7, 17, 23–24, 25
and Menelaus, 62
role in the Trojan War, 18, 24
and the Trojan horse, 61
Hellenistic Age, 12
Hephaestus, 48, 53
Hera, 19–22, 27, 37, 45, 53
Heracles, 27, 58, 63
Hermes, 21–22, 51, 87, 89, 91, 93, 100
Homer, 5, 12, 13–15, 74–75
hubris (pride), 13, 29, 38, 118

I

Iliad
authorship, 13–15
basic plot, 5, 7
existing sites from, 10
publication, 15
structure, 29
themes, 30–31, 42, 116
Ilium, 29, 118. *See also* Troy
Iphigenia, 31–32
Iris, 51, 52
Island of the Sun, 91, 93, 96, 99, 103
Ithaca, 7, 8, 69, 74, 91, 108

J

Jason and the Argonauts, 96

K

kleos (glory), 31, 118

L

Laertes, 110, 114
Laestrygonians, 88, 93
Laocoön, 61, 64, 65
lays, 14, 118
Lotus-Eaters, 69–75
Lucian, 18
Lycians, 30
Lycomedes, 43

M

Menelaus of Sparta, King
action against Paris, 17, 24, 25
combat with Paris, 36–37, 41
marriage to Helen, 23, 62
and Telemachus, 110
and the Trojan horse, 58, 62
Minoans, 9, 10
moly (antidote), 87, 118
Myceneans and Mycenaean Age, 9–11
Myrmidons, 36, 46

N

Neoptolemus, 55, 57, 61–62
Nestor, 10, 37, 38–39, 110
Nostoi, 11, 67, 118
nymph, 119

O

Odysseus
in Agamemnon's war with Achilles, 37, 38, 43
anti-Odysseus tradition, 74, 85
characteristics, 67, 85, 104–105
and Charybdis, 96, 98, 103, 105
and Circe, 87, 88–94
claiming Achilles' armor, 57, 63
and the Cyclops, 77–85
fighting Trojans, 56
and the Lotus-Eaters, 69–75
return home, 107–117
and Scylla, 96, 98, 103, 104
and the Sirens, 96, 97, 103, 104
and the Trojan horse, 55, 57–58, 60, 63-64
Odyssey
authorship, 5, 13–15, 87
basic plot, 7, 67, 116
book production, 15, 119
existing sites from, 10
link to folktales, 94, 117
themes, 67–68, 77, 94, 116, 117

P

Palladium, 57, 58, 60, 63
Paris
combat with Menelaus, 36–37, 41

death, 58
the judgment of, 22–27
kidnapping of Helen, 7, 16,
23–24, 25
killing of Achilles, 56, 63
recommendation by Zeus,
19–21, 25
Patroclus, 36, 38, 39–40, 41, 46,
50, 57, 92
Peleus, 19, 29, 53
Peloponnesian War, 12
Penelope, 92
characteristics, 116–117
Odysseus homesick for, 69, 96,
100, 102, 104
during return of Odysseus, 107,
109–117
Phaeacians, 68, 105, 107, 114
Philoetius, 111, 113, 115
polis (city-state), 11, 12, 26, 42,
119
Polyphemus (Cyclops), 77–85
Poseidon
and Athena releasing
Odysseus, 100
destruction of Odysseus' ships,
69, 73, 108, 114
father of Cyclops, 82, 83
punishment of the Phaeacians,
107
Priam, 18, 21, 30, 51, 52, 61–62

R
religion, 13
Romans and Roman Empire, 12,
74

S
Sarpedon, 13
Scylla, 96, 98, 103, 104
Sinon, 60, 61, 64, 65
Sirens, 96, 97, 103, 104
Sparta, 12, 107, 110

T
Telemachus, 43, 69, 96
on Odysseus' return home,
111, 113, 115

in Pylos and Sparta, 107, 109,
114
theomachies, 45, 119
Thetis
in Achilles' battle with Hector,
46, 48, 50–51, 53
making Achilles immortal, 31
mourning Achilles, 55, 56–57,
63
Tiresias, 91–92, 93
Trojan Cycle, 17
Trojan horse, 55–65
Trojans
in Achilles' argument with
Agamemnon, 30, 37
in Achilles' battle with Hector,
46–53
discussing the horse, 58, 60–61
Trojan War
cause, 5, 7, 8, 13, 18, 24, 25
peoples involved, 30, 42
Trojan Women, 18, 55
Troy
legendary, 17
the real, 7–8, 10, 26, 30
Tyndareus, King, 22–23

U
Underworld, 31, 55, 91, 93

V
Virgil, 55

X
xenia (guest-friendship), 18, 25,
27, 84, 94, 107, 109

Z
Zeus
anger toward Achilles, 50–51,
52
domain, 13
on doom of Hector, 40
promise to Thetis, 36, 37
recommending Paris as judge,
19–21, 25
release of Odysseus, 101–102,
108
revenge on Odysseus, 99, 100,
103